STANDARDS PRACTICE BOOK

For Home or School

Grade K

INCLUDES:

- Home or School Practice
- Lesson Practice and Test Preparation
- English and Spanish School-Home Letters
- Dig Deeper and Connect Lessons
- Getting Ready for Grade 1 Lessons

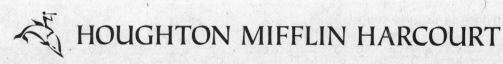

HOUGHTON MIFFLIN HARCOURT

Number and Operations

Big Idea Project B1

1 Model, Read and Write Numbers 0 to 5

School-Home Letter (English) P1
School-Home Letter (Spanish) P2
1.1   **Hands On:** Model 1 and 2 . . . . P3
1.2   Read and Write 1 and 2 . . . . P5
1.3   **Hands On:** Model 3 and 4 . . . . P7
1.4   Read and Write 3 and 4 . . . . P9
1.5   **Hands On:** Model 5 . . . . P11
1.6   Read and Write 5 . . . . P13
1.7   **Problem Solving:** Make a Model · Zero. P15
1.8   Read and Write 0 . . . . P17
      Extra Practice P19

2 Compare and Order Numbers to 5

School-Home Letter (English) P21
School-Home Letter (Spanish) P22
2.1   **Hands On:** Same Number P23
2.2   **Hands On:** One More P25
2.3   **Hands On:** One Fewer P27
2.4   **Hands On:** Compare Sets P29
2.5   **Problem Solving:** Make a Model ·
      Compare Numbers to 5 . . . . P31
2.6   **Hands On:** Order Numbers to 5 . . . . P33
2.7   Ordinal Numbers to 5th P35
      Extra Practice P37

3

Represent, Compare, and Order Numbers 6 to 10

School-Home Letter (English) P39

School-Home Letter (Spanish) P40

3.1 **Hands On:** Model 6 . . . . P41

3.2 Read and Write 6 . . . . P43

3.3 **Hands On:** Model 7 . . . . P45

3.4 Read and Write 7 . . . . P47

3.5 **Hands On:** Model 8 . . . . P49

3.6 Read and Write 8 . . . . P51

3.7 **Hands On:** Model 9 . . . . P53

3.8 Read and Write 9 . . . . P55

3.9 **Hands On:** Model 10 . . . . P57

3.10 Read and Write 10 . . . . P59

3.10A **DIG DEEPER** How Many Ones? P60a

3.11 **Hands On:** Algebra • Ways to Make 10 . . . . P61

3.12 **Problem Solving:** Make a Model • Compare Numbers to 10 . . . . P63

3.13 Count Forward to 10 . . . . P65

3.14 Count Backward from 10 . . . . P67

Extra Practice P69

© Houghton Mifflin Harcourt Publishing Company

4 Addition and Subtraction

School-Home Letter (English) P71
School-Home Letter (Spanish) P72

4.1 **Problem Solving:** Act It Out • Joining Problems P73

4.2 **Hands On:** Algebra • Model Joining P75

4.3 **Algebra:** Join Sets P77

4.4 **Algebra:** Introduce Symbols to Add P79

4.4A **CONNECT** Addition Expressions P80a

4.5 **Algebra:** Addition Sentences P81

4.5A **DIG DEEPER Algebra:** Break Apart a Set P82a

4.6 **Hands On:** Algebra • Add Equal Sets P83

4.7 **Hands On:** Algebra • Create and Model
Addition Problems P85

4.8 **Problem Solving:** Act It Out • Separating Problems P87

4.9 **Hands On:** Algebra • Model Separating. P89

4.10 **Algebra:** Separate Sets P91

4.11 **Algebra:** Introduce Symbols to Subtract P93

4.11A **CONNECT** Subtraction Expressions P94a

4.11B **CONNECT** Equal To. P94c

4.12 **Algebra:** Subtraction Sentences P95

4.13 **Hands On:** Algebra • Create and Model
Subtraction Problems. P97

4.14 **Hands On:** Algebra • Addition and Subtraction P99

Extra Practice. P101

© Houghton Mifflin Harcourt Publishing Company

5   Model, Read, and Write 11 to 19

School-Home Letter (English) P103
School-Home Letter (Spanish) P104
5.1   **Hands On:** Model 11 and 12 . . . . P105
    5.1A   **CONNECT** Build 10 and Complete the Equation P106a
    5.1B   **DIG DEEPER** Take Apart 10 and Complete the Equation P106c
5.2   Read and Write 11 and 12 . . . . P107
5.3   **Hands On:** Model 13 and 14 . . . . P109
5.4   Read and Write 13 and 14 . . . . P111
5.5   **Hands On:** Understand 15 . . . . P113
5.6   **Problem Solving:** Draw a Picture · Fifteen P115
5.7   **Hands On:** Model 16 and 17 . . . . P117
5.8   Read and Write 16 and 17 . . . . P119
5.9   **Hands On:** Model 18 and 19 . . . . P121
5.10   Read and Write 18 and 19 . . . . P123
    5.10A   **DIG DEEPER** Compare Numbers to 9 with Teen Numbers . . . P124a
    5.10B   **DIG DEEPER** Compare and Order Teen Numbers P124c
    5.10C   **DIG DEEPER** Build and Break Apart Teen Numbers P124e
Extra Practice P125

6   Numbers to 20 and Beyond

School-Home Letter (English) P127
School-Home Letter (Spanish) P128
6.1   **Hands On:** Model 20 . . . . P129
6.2   Read and Write 20 . . . . P131
6.3   **Problem Solving:** Make a Model ·
Compare Numbers to 20 . . . . P133
6.4   Count and Order Numbers to 20 . . . . P135
6.5   Count Forward and Backward P137
6.6   Numbers 21 to 31 . . . . P139
6.7   Count to 100 . . . . P141
6.8   Use a Hundred Chart P143
    6.8A   **DIG DEEPER** Counting Tens P144a
    6.8B   **DIG DEEPER** Tens and Ones P144c
Extra Practice P145

© Houghton Mifflin Harcourt Publishing Company

Geometry, Data, and Patterns

Big Idea Project **B3**

7 Sorting and Data

School-Home Letter (English) P147
School-Home Letter (Spanish) P148
7.1 **Hands On:** Algebra · Sort and Describe by Color P149
7.2 **Hands On:** Algebra · Sort and Describe by Shape P151
7.3 **Hands On:** Algebra · Sort and Describe by Size P153
7.4 **Problem Solving:** Make a Graph · Concrete Graphs P155
7.5 Read a Picture Graph P157
7.6 Make a Picture Graph P159
Extra Practice P161

8 Two-Dimensional Shapes

School-Home Letter (English) P163
School-Home Letter (Spanish) P164
8.1 Identify and Name Squares P165
8.2 Describe Squares P167
8.3 Identify and Name Triangles P169
8.4 Describe Triangles P171
8.5 Identify and Name Circles P173
8.6 Describe Circles P175
8.7 Identify and Name Rectangles P177
8.8 Describe Rectangles P179
8.9 **Hands On:** Algebra · Sort
Two-Dimensional Shapes P181
8.10 **Hands On:** Identify and Describe Other Shapes P183
8.11 **Problem Solving:** Draw a Picture ·
Combine Shapes P185
8.12 Symmetry P187
Extra Practice P189

9 Positions and Patterns

School-Home Letter (English) P191
School-Home Letter (Spanish) P192
9.1 **Hands On:** Above, Below, Over, and Under P193
9.2 **Hands On:** Beside, Next to, and Between P195
9.3 **Hands On:** Algebra · Describe and Copy a
Color Pattern P197
9.4 **Hands On:** Algebra · Describe and Copy a
Size Pattern P199
9.5 **Hands On:** Algebra · Describe and Copy a
Shape Pattern P201
9.6 **Problem Solving:** Find a Pattern ·
Number Patterns P203
9.7 **Hands On:** Algebra · Extend a Shape Pattern P205
9.8 **Algebra:** Extend a Size Pattern P207
9.9 **Algebra:** Extend a Number Pattern P209
9.10 **Hands On:** Algebra · Describe and
Copy a Growing Pattern P211
9.11 **Hands On:** Algebra · Create a Pattern P213
Extra Practice P215

10 Three-Dimensional Shapes

School-Home Letter (English) P217
School-Home Letter (Spanish) P218
10.1 Identify and Describe Spheres P219
10.2 Identify and Describe Cubes P221
10.3 Identify and Describe Cylinders P223
10.4 Identify and Describe Cones P225
10.5 Identify and Describe Pyramids P227
10.6 Identify and Describe Rectangular Prisms P229
10.7 **Problem Solving:** Draw a Picture · Sort Shapes P231
Extra Practice P233

Measurement and Money

Big Idea Project **B5**

11 Measurement

School-Home Letter (English) **P235**
School-Home Letter (Spanish) **P236**
11.1 **Hands On:** Compare Lengths **P237**
11.2 **Hands On:** Order Lengths **P239**
11.3 **Hands On:** Compare Lengths
Using Nonstandard Units **P241**
11.4 **Hands On:** Compare Heights **P243**
11.5 **Problem Solving:** Draw a Picture • Order Heights **P245**
11.6 **Hands On:** Compare and Order Weights **P247**
11.6A **DIG DEEPER** Length, Height, and Weight **P248a**
11.6B **DIG DEEPER** Explore Capacity **P248c**
Extra Practice **P249**

12 Money

School-Home Letter (English) **P251**
School-Home Letter (Spanish) **P252**
12.1 **Hands On:** Penny **P253**
12.2 **Hands On:** Nickel **P255**
12.3 **Hands On:** Dime **P257**
12.4 **Hands On:** Quarter **P259**
12.5 **Problem Solving:** Draw a Picture • Use Coins **P261**
Extra Practice **P263**

End-of-Year Resources

Getting Ready for Grade 1

These lessons review important skills and prepare you for Grade 1.

Lesson 1	**Hands On:** Add One	**P265**
Lesson 2	Add Two	**P267**
Lesson 3	**Hands On:** Add on a Ten Frame	**P269**
Lesson 4	Part-Part-Whole	**P271**
Lesson 5	Addition Sentences	**P273**
Checkpoint		**P275**
Lesson 6	**Hands On:** Subtract One	**P277**
Lesson 7	Subtract Two	**P279**
Lesson 8	**Hands On:** Subtract on a Ten Frame	**P281**
Lesson 9	**Algebra:** Missing Part	**P283**
Lesson 10	Subtraction Sentences	**P285**
Lesson 11	Subtract to Compare	**P287**
Checkpoint		**P289**
Lesson 12	Order Numbers to 30	**P291**
Lesson 13	**Hands On:** Skip Count by Twos	**P293**
Lesson 14	**Hands On:** Skip Count by Fives	**P295**
Lesson 15	Tally Marks	**P297**
Lesson 16	Skip Count by Tens	**P299**
Lesson 17	Skip Count Coins	**P301**
Checkpoint		**P303**
Lesson 18	**Hands On:** Algebra · Extend a Growing Pattern	**P305**
Lesson 19	Explore Measuring Tools	**P307**
Lesson 20	Use a Clock	**P309**
Checkpoint		**P311**

School-Home Letter

Dear Family,

My class started Chapter 1 today. In this chapter, I will use pictures, numbers, and words to show 0 to 5.

Love, _____

Vocabulary

one a number for a single object

two one more than one

Home Activity

Use this five frame and counters, such as beans or buttons. Have your child place counters on the five frame to show the numbers 0–5. For 0, have your child place one counter on the five frame, and then remove it. Together practice writing the numbers 0–5.

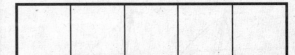

Literature

Look for these books in a library. These books will reinforce your child's counting skills.

Counting
Barefoot Books, 2006.

Fish Eyes
by Lois Ehlert. Voyager Books, 1992.

Carta
para la casa

Querida familia:

Mi clase comenzó hoy el Capítulo 1. En este capítulo, usaré imágenes, números y palabras para mostrar del 0 al 5.

Con cariño, _____

Vocabulario

uno el número de un solo objeto

dos uno más que uno

Actividad para la casa

Use este cuadro de cinco y fichas como botones o frijoles. Pida a su hijo que ponga las fichas en el cuadro para mostrar los números de 0 a 5. Para 0, pídale que coloque una ficha en el cuadro de cinco y luego que la quite. Juntos, practiquen la escritura de los números de 0 a 5.

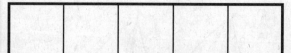

Literatura

Busquen estos libros en la biblioteca. Estos libros ayudarán a su hijo a reforzar la destreza de contar.

Counting
Barefoot Books, 2006.

Fish Eyes
por Lois Ehlert
Voyager Books, 1992.

Name _____

Model 1 and 2

 1

2
two

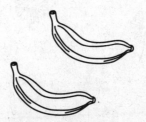

 2

1
one

 3

2
two

 4

1
one

DIRECTIONS 1–4. Use cubes to show the number of objects. Say the number. Draw the cubes.

Lesson Check

Spiral Review

DIRECTIONS **1.** Which group shows 2 objects? Mark under your answer. **(Lesson 1.1)** **2.** Which group shows 1 object? Mark under your answer. **(Lesson 1.1)** **3.** Which group shows 2 objects? Mark under your answer. **(Lesson 1.1)**

Name _____

Read and Write I and 2

DIRECTIONS I–4. Count and tell how many. Write the number.

Lesson Check

1	3	2	4
○	○	○	○

Spiral Review

○	○	○	○

○	○	○	○

DIRECTIONS **1.** Count and tell how many cubes. Mark under your answer. **(Lesson 1.2)** **2.** Which group shows 2 objects? Mark under your answer. **(Lesson 1.1)** **3.** Which group shows 1 object? Mark under your answer. **(Lesson 1.1)**

Name _____

Model 3 and 4

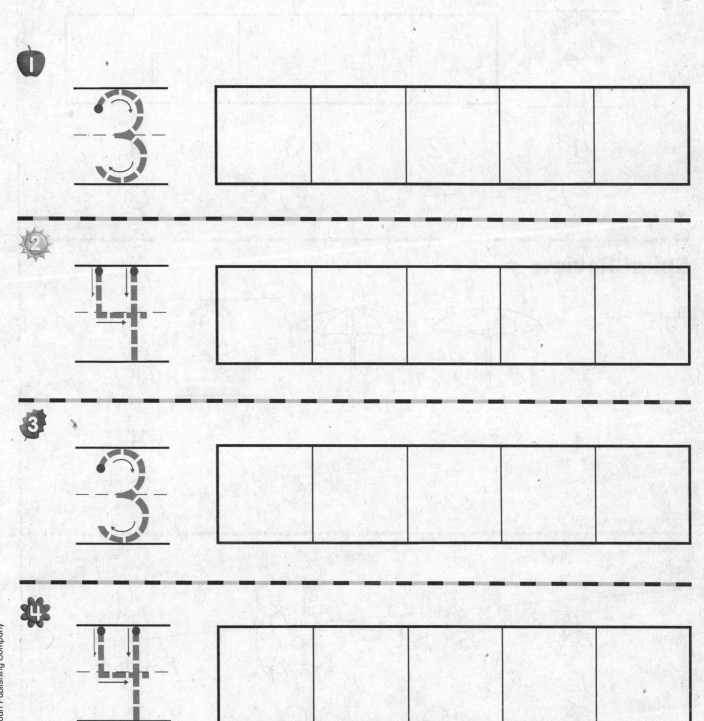

DIRECTIONS 1–4. Place counters in the five frame to show the number. Draw the counters. Trace the number.

© Houghton Mifflin Harcourt Publishing Company

Lesson Check

1   2   3   4

○   ○   ○   ○

Spiral Review

1   2   3   4

○   ○   ○   ○

○   ○   ○   ○

DIRECTIONS   **1.** How many counters would you put in the five frame? Mark under your answer. **(Lesson 1.3)**   **2.** Count and tell how many umbrellas. Mark under your answer. **(Lesson 1.2)**   **3.** Which group shows 1 object? Mark under your answer. **(Lesson 1.1)**

Name _____

Read and Write 3 and 4

1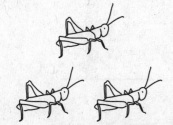

3

2

_____

_ _ _ _ _ _ _ _

_____

3

_____

_ _ _ _ _ _ _ _

_____

4

_____

_ _ _ _ _ _ _ _

_____

5

_____

_ _ _ _ _ _ _ _

_____

6

_____

_ _ _ _ _ _ _ _

_____

DIRECTIONS 1–6. Count and tell how many. Write the number.

Chapter 1

Lesson Check

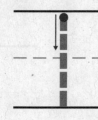   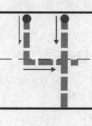

○   ○   ○   ○

Spiral Review

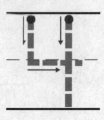 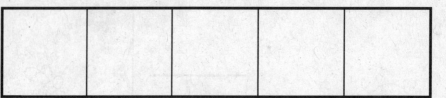

○   ○   ○   ○

1   2   3   4

○   ○   ○   ○

DIRECTIONS 1. Count and tell how many butterflies. Mark under your answer. (Lesson 1.4) 2. How many counters would you put in the five frame? Mark under your answer. (Lesson 1.3) 3. Count and tell how many flowers. Mark under your answer. (Lesson 1.2)

Name _____

Model 5

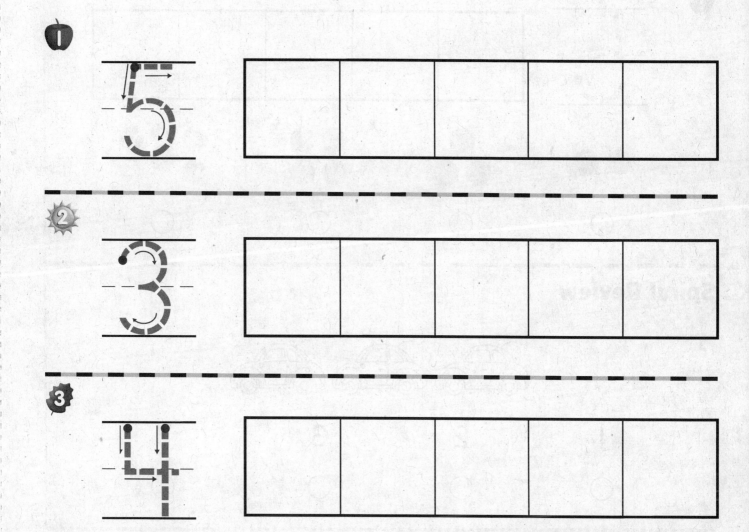

DIRECTIONS 1. Place counters to show five. Draw the counters.
Trace the number. 2. Place counters to show three. Draw the
counters. Trace the number. 3. Place counters to show four. Draw
the counters. Trace the number. 4. Place counters to show five.
Draw the counters. Trace the number.

  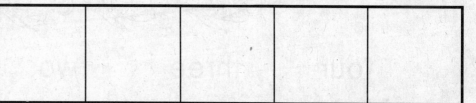

Lesson Check

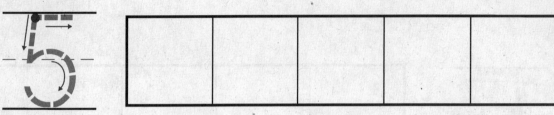

○　　　　　○　　　　　○　　　　　○

Spiral Review

| 1 | 2 | 3 | 4 |

○　　　　　○　　　　　○　　　　　○

| four | three | two | one |

○　　　　　○　　　　　○　　　　　○

DIRECTIONS 1. How many counters would you place in the five frame? Mark under your answer. (Lesson 1.5) 2. Count and tell how many race cars. Mark under your answer. (Lesson 1.4) 3. Count and tell how many fish. Mark under your answer. (Lesson 1.4)

Name _____

Read and Write 5

1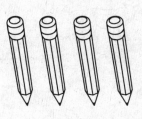

_____

\- - - - - - - - -

_____

2

_____

\- - - - - - - - -

3

_____

\- - - - - - - - -

_____

4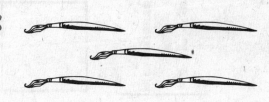

_____

\- - - - - - - - -

_____

5

_____

\- - - - - - - - -

6

_____

\- - - - - - - - -

DIRECTIONS 1–6. Write the number that shows how many objects are in the set.

Chapter 1

Lesson Check

2	3	4	5
○	○	○	○

Spiral Review

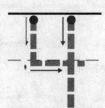 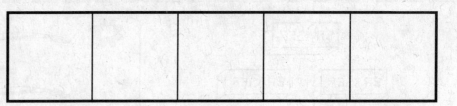

5	4	2	1
○	○	○	○

DIRECTIONS 1. Count and tell how many animals. Mark under your answer. (Lesson 1.6) 2. How many counters would you place in the five frame? Mark under your answer. (Lesson 1.3) 3. Count and tell how many pieces of pepperoni. Mark under your answer. (Lesson 1.2)

P14 fourteen

Make a Model • Zero

———
- - -
———

- -

2

———
- - -
———

DIRECTIONS Use counters to model the problems. **1.** Oliver has one juice box. Lucy has one juice box fewer than Oliver. How many juice boxes does Lucy have? Write the number. **2.** Jessica does not have a book to read. Wesley has 2 more books than Jessica. How many books does Wesley have? Write the number.

Lesson Check

0	1	2	3
○	○	○	○

Spiral Review

2	3	4	5
○	○	○	○

0	1	2	3
○	○	○	○

DIRECTIONS 1. Eva has 2 apples in her basket. She eats 1 apple and gives 1 to Sam. How many apples does Eva have now? Mark under your answer. (Lesson 1.7) 2. Count and tell how many cubes. Mark under your answer. (Lesson 1.4) 3. Count and tell how many squirrels. Mark under your answer. (Lesson 1.2)

P16 sixteen

© Houghton Mifflin Harcourt Publishing Company

Name _____

Read and Write 0

DIRECTIONS 1–4. Write the number to show how many birds are in the cage. Circle the cages that have 0 birds.

Lesson Check

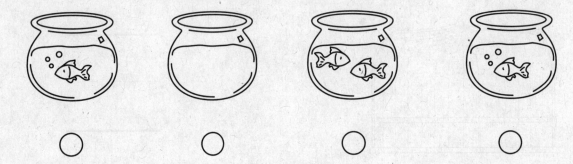

○   ○   ○   ○

Spiral Review

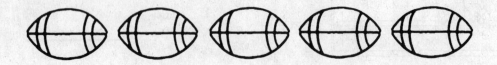

2   3   4   5

○   ○   ○   ○

○   ○   ○   ○

DIRECTIONS   1. Which bowl has 0 fish? Mark under your answer.
(Lesson 1.8)   2. Count and tell how many footballs. Mark under your
answer. **(Lesson 1.6)   3.** Which group shows 5 objects? Mark under
your answer. **(Lesson 1.5)**

P18 eighteen

Chapter 1 Extra Practice

Lessons 1.1 – 1.4 (pp. 5 – 19) ·

one

· ·

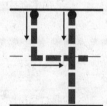

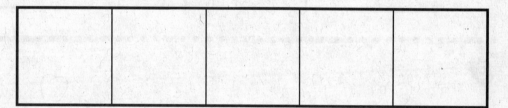

· ·

3

_____

- - - - - - - - - - -

_____

4

_____

- - - - - - - - - - -

_____

· ·

5

_____

- - - - - - - - - - -

_____

6

_____

- - - - - - - - - - -

_____

DIRECTIONS **1.** Use cubes to show the number of objects. Say the number. Draw the cubes. Trace the number. **2.** Place counters in the five frame to show the number. Draw the counters. Trace the number. **3–6.** Count and tell how many. Write the number.

1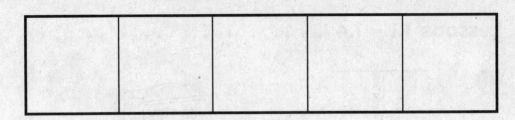

2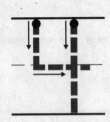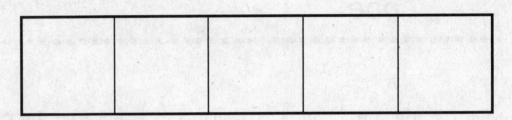

3

4

5

DIRECTIONS **1.** Place counters to show five. Draw the counters. Trace the number. **2.** Place counters to show four. Draw the counters. Trace the number. **3.** Circle the sets of five apples. **4–5.** Write the number to show how many birds are in the cage. Circle the cage that has 0 birds.

P20 twenty

School-Home **Letter**

Dear Family,

My class started Chapter 2 today. We will learn how to show more and fewer with numbers and counters. I will also learn how to compare and order sets to 5.

Love, _____

Vocabulary

same number alike in number or amount

○ There are the same number
△ of counters and triangles.

more greater in number or amount

○○○ There are more counters
△△ than triangles.

fewer smaller in number or amount

○ There are fewer counters
△△ than triangles.

Home Activity

Gather items that your child can easily hold and move, and line them up on a table in two groups of different quantities. Ask your child to count and tell you how many are in the set with more and how many are in the set with fewer.

Then change the number in each group and have your child show different ways to show sets with more and fewer objects.

Literature

Look for these books in the library. They will help reinforce the concepts of more and fewer.

More, Fewer, Less by Tana Hoban. Greenwillow, 1998.

Henry the Fourth by Stuart J. Murphy. HarperTrophy, 1998.

Querida familia:

Mi clase comenzó hoy el Capítulo 2. Aprenderemos cómo mostrar más y menos con números y fichas. También aprénderé cómo comparar y ordenar conjuntos hasta 5.

Con cariño, _____

Vocabulario

número igual el mismo número o cantidad

○ Hay un número igual de
△ fichas que de triángulos.

más mayor en número o cantidad

○○○ Hay más fichas que
△△ triángulos.

menos menor en número o cantidad

○ Hay menos fichas que
△△ triángulos.

Actividad para la casa

Reúna objetos que su hijo pueda sostener o mover fácilmente y colóquelos en fila sobre una mesa en dos conjuntos de diferentes cantidades. Pida a su hijo que los cuente y le diga cuántos hay en el grupo que tiene más y cuántos en el grupo que tiene menos.

Luego cambie el número en cada conjunto y pida a su hijo que le muestre distintas maneras de formar conjuntos con más o con menos objetos.

Literatura

Busquen estos libros en la biblioteca. Estos libros ayudarán a su hijo a reforzar los conceptos de más y menos.

More, Fewer, Less
por Tana Hoban. Greenwillow, 1998.

Henry the Fourth
por Stuart J. Murphy. Harper Trophy, 1998.

Name _____

Same Number

_____

- - - - - -

_____

- - - - - -

_____

_____

- - - - - -

_____

_____

- - - - - -

_____

DIRECTIONS I–2. Place a cube below each object to show the same number of objects. Draw and color each cube. Compare the sets of objects. Write how many objects are in each row.

Lesson Check

 ○    ○    ○    ○

Spiral Review

○   ○   ○   ○

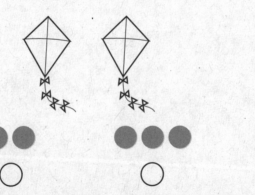

●   ○   ● ●   ○   ● ● ●   ○   ● ● ● ●   ○

DIRECTIONS   1. How many toys are needed to make a set with the same number? Mark under your answer. **(Lesson 2.1)   2.** Mark under the bird cage that has 0 birds. **(Lesson 1.7)   3.** Count and tell how many kites. Mark under the set of counters that shows the number. **(Lesson 1.1)**

Name _____

One More

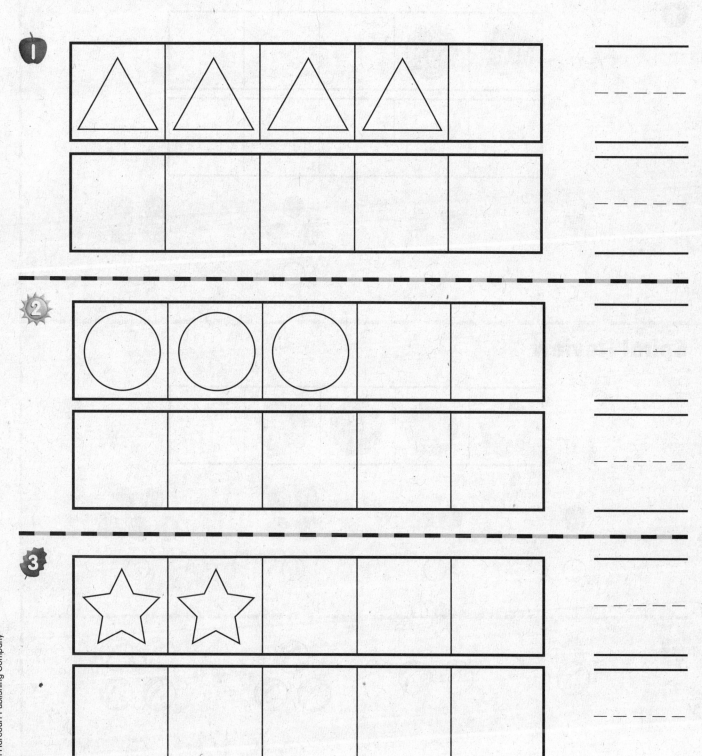

DIRECTIONS 1–3. Count and tell how many. Write the number. Create a set that has one more shape. Draw the shapes. Write how many.

Chapter 2

twenty-five **P25**

Lesson Check

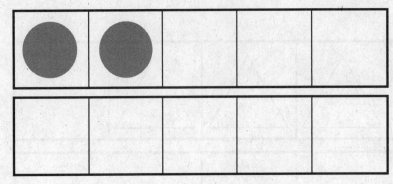

○   ○   ○   ○

Spiral Review

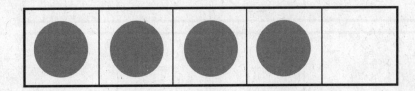

○   ○   ○   ○

○   ○   ○   ○

DIRECTIONS 1. How many counters make a set with one more counter? Mark under your answer. **(Lesson 2.2) 2.** How many counters? Mark under your answer. **(Lesson 1.3) 3.** Which group shows 2 objects? Mark under your answer. **(Lesson 1.1)**

P26 twenty-six

© Houghton Mifflin Harcourt Publishing Company

Name _____

One Fewer

 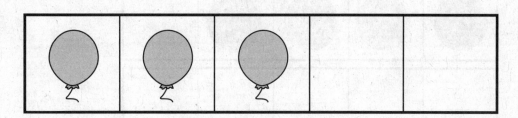

- -

 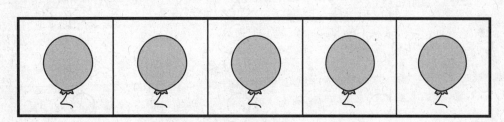

DIRECTIONS I–2. Count and tell how many. Write the number. Create a set that has one fewer balloon. Draw the balloons. Write how many.

Chapter 2

twenty-seven **P27**

Lesson Check

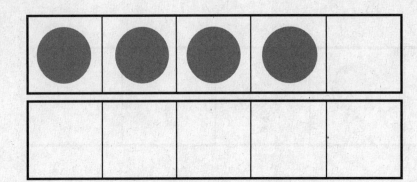

○   ○   ○   ○

Spiral Review

○   ○   ○   ○

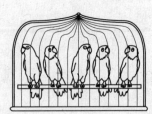

2   3   4   5

○   ○   ○   ○

DIRECTIONS 1. How many counters? Mark under the set that shows one fewer counter. (Lesson 2.3)   2. Which group shows four objects? Mark under your answer. (Lesson 1.3)   3. Count how many birds. Mark under your answer. (Lesson 1.6)

P28 twenty-eight

Name _____

Compare Sets

_____
- - - - - - - - - - -
_____
_____

- -

_____
- - - - - - - - - - -
_____
_____

- -

_____
- - - - - - - - - - -
_____
_____

DIRECTIONS 1–3. Count and tell how many balls. Write the number. Use counters to create a set that has a different number than the set of balls. Draw the counters. Write how many. Compare the sets.

Lesson Check

○   ○   ○   ○

Spiral Review

○   ○   ○   ○

1   2   3   4

○   ○   ○   ○

DIRECTIONS   **1.** How many sailboats? Compare the set in the five frame with the sets below. Mark under the set that shows fewer sailboats. (Lesson 2.4)   **2.** Which group shows 3 objects? Mark under your answer. (Lesson 1.3)   **3.** Which is the number three? Mark under your answer. (Lesson 1.4)

Make a Model • Compare Numbers to 5

 1

_____
- - - - - - - - - -
_____

_____
- - - - - - - - - -
_____

 2

_____
- - - - - - - - - -
_____

_____
- - - - - - - - - -
_____

DIRECTIONS **1.** How many apples? Write the number. Use cubes to create a set with more than 2 objects. Draw the cubes. Write how many. **2.** Count and tell how many crayons. Use cubes to create a set with fewer than 5 objects. Draw the cubes. Write how many.

Lesson Check

○   ○   ○   ○

Spiral Review

 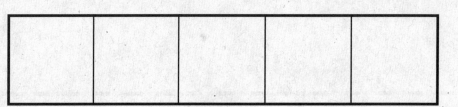

 ○   ○   ○   ○

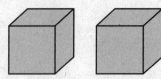

1   2   3   4

○   ○   ○   ○

DIRECTIONS   1. Which set has fewer bears than the set shown? Mark under your answer. **(Lesson 2.5)   2.** How many counters would you put in the five frame? Mark under your answer. **(Lesson 1.5)   3.** How many blocks? Mark under your answer. **(Lesson 1.1)**

Order Numbers to 5

- -

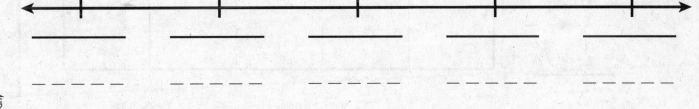

DIRECTIONS 1. Write how many flowers are in each vase.
2. Write those numbers in order on the number line.

Lesson Check

1, 2, 3, 4, 5   2, 1, 3, 4, 5   3, 2, 1, 4, 5   5, 4, 1, 2, 3

○   ○   ○   ○

Spiral Review

2   3   4   5

○   ○   ○   ○

 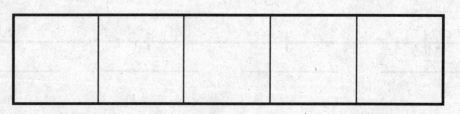

DIRECTIONS 1. Which set of numbers is in order? Mark under your answer. **(Lesson 2.6)** 2. How many are in the set of stars? Mark under your answer. **(Lesson 1.4)** 3. How many counters would you put in the five frame? Mark under your answer. **(Lesson 1.4)**

Ordinal Numbers to 5th

first

first

first

first

DIRECTIONS I. Circle the first duck. Draw a line under the fifth duck.
2. Circle the second dog. Draw a line under the fifth dog.   3. Circle
the third sheep. Draw a line under the fourth sheep.   4. Circle the first turtle.
Draw a line under the fourth turtle.

Lesson Check

1

first

Spiral Review

2

1   2   4   5

DIRECTIONS **1.** Which sailboat is fourth in line? Mark under your answer. (Lesson 2.7) **2.** Count how many blocks. Mark under your answer. (Lesson 1.6) **3.** Which group shows three trucks? Mark under your answer. (Lesson 1.3)

P36 thirty-six

Chapter 2 Extra Practice

Lessons 2.1 – 2.4 (pp. 53 – 68) · · · · · · · · · · · · · · · ·

_____

- - - - - - - -

═══════════

 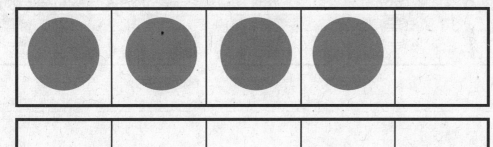

_____

- - - - - - - -

_____

- - - - - - - -

_____

DIRECTIONS **I.** Place a cube below each object to show the same number of objects. Draw and color each cube. Write how many objects are in each row. **2.** Count and tell how many. Write the number. Create a set that has one more counter. Draw the counters. Write how many. **3.** Count and tell how many suns. Write the number. Use counters to show a set that has fewer counters than the set of suns. Draw the counters. Write how many. Compare the sets.

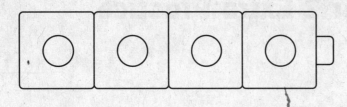

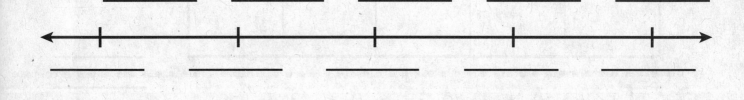

first

DIRECTIONS **1.** Count and tell how many cubes. Write the number. Create a cube train that has fewer than 4 cubes. Draw the cube train. Write how many. **2.** Write how many flowers are in each flower pot. Write those numbers in order on the number line. **3.** Circle the second dog. Mark an X on the fourth dog. Draw a line under the fifth dog.

P38 thirty-eight

School-Home Letter

Dear Family,

My class started Chapter 3 today. In this chapter I will use pictures, numbers, and words to show 6 to 10.

Love, _____

Vocabulary

six one more than five

eight one more than seven

Home Activity

Pour salt or sand into a cookie sheet or baking dish. Pick a number from 6 to 10 and have your child draw the number in the salt/sand. Then ask your child to draw circles to match that number. Shake to erase and begin again!

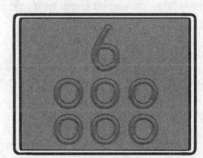

Literature

Look for these books in the library. You and your child will enjoy these fun stories while learning more about the numbers 6 to 10.

Seven Scary Monsters by Mary Beth Lundgren. Clarion Books, 2003.

Ten Black Dots by Donald Crews. HarperTrophy, 1995.

Carta
para la casa

Querida familia:

Mi clase comenzó hoy el Capítulo 3. En este capítulo, usaré ilustraciones, números y palabras para mostrar los números del 6 al 10.

Con cariño, _____

Vocabulario

seis uno más que cinco

ocho uno más que siete

Actividad para la casa

Ponga sal o arena en una bandeja de pastelería o en una bandeja de vidrio para hornear. Elija un número del 6 al 10 y pida a su hijo que dibuje el número en la sal o arena. Luego pídale que dibuje el mismo número de círculos. Mezcle para borrar y ¡comiencen de nuevo!

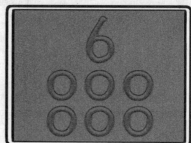

Literatura

Busquen estos libros en la biblioteca. Usted y su hijo se divertirán leyendo estos cuentos mientras aprenden más sobre los números del 6 al 10.

Seven Scary Monsters
por Mary Beth Lundgren.
Clarion Books, 2003.

Los diez puntos negros
por Donald Crews.
Harper Trophy, 1995.

Model 6

six

- -

_____

six

DIRECTIONS **I.** Use counters to show the number. Draw the counters. Trace the number. **2.** Use counters to show the number. Draw the counters. Write the number.

Lesson Check

1

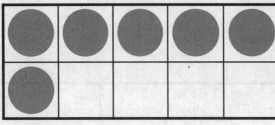

3   4   5   6

○   ○   ○   ○

Spiral Review

2

○   ○   ○   ○

3

1   2   3   4

○   ○   ○   ○

DIRECTIONS   **I.** How many counters? Mark under your answer.
(Lesson 3.1)   **2.** Count and tell how many counters are in the five frame.
Mark under the set of counters that shows one fewer counter.
(Lesson 2.3)   **3.** How many cubes? Mark under your answer.   (Lesson 1.4)

Read and Write 6

6
six

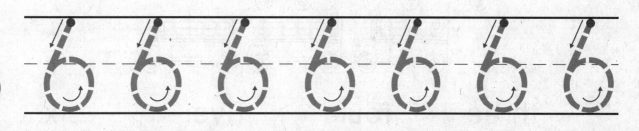

_____

_ _ _ _ _ _ _ _

_____

_____

_ _ _ _ _ _ _ _

_____

_____

_ _ _ _ _ _ _ _

_____

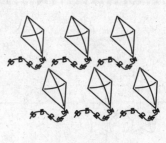

_____

_ _ _ _ _ _ _ _

_____

DIRECTIONS **1.** Say the number. Trace the numbers.
2–5. Count and tell how many. Write the number.

Lesson Check

three	four	five	six
○	○	○	○

Spiral Review

○ ○ ○ ○

○ ○ ○ ○

DIRECTIONS **1.** How many school buses? Mark under your answer.
(Lesson 3.2) **2.** Count and tell how many counters are in the five frame.
Mark under the set of counters that shows one more counter. (Lesson 2.2)
3. Which group shows two objects? Mark under your answer. (Lesson 1.1)

P44 forty-four

© Houghton Mifflin Harcourt Publishing Company

Name _____

Model 7

 1

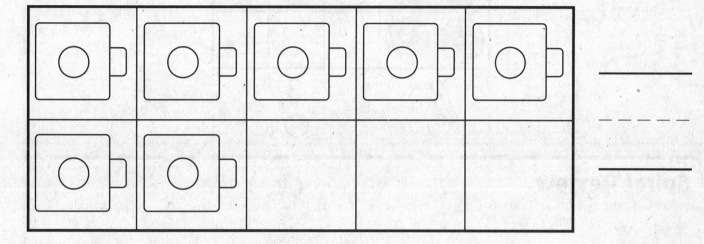

_____

_ _ _

_____

 2

_____

_ _ _

7 is ___ less than 10

 3

DIRECTIONS 1. Place cubes on the ones in the ten frame. Tell how many cubes. Write the number. 2. How many less than 10 is 7? Write the number. 3. Circle the sets that have 7 pumpkins.

Chapter 3

forty-five **P45**

Lesson Check

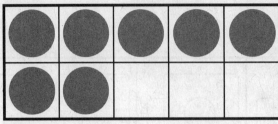

1   2   3   4

○   ○   ○   ○

Spiral Review

first

○   ○   ○   ○

1   2   3   4

○   ○   ○   ○

DIRECTIONS **1.** How many more than 5 is 7? Mark under your answer. (Lesson 3.3) **2.** Which person is second in line? Mark under your answer. (Lesson 2.7) **3.** How many birds? Mark under your answer. (Lesson 1.4)

Name _____

Read and Write 7

7
seven

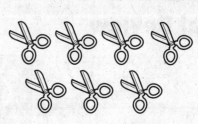

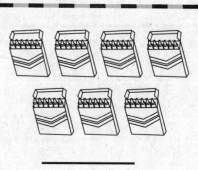

DIRECTIONS **1.** Say the number. Trace the numbers.
2–5. Count and tell how many. Write the number.

Lesson Check

1

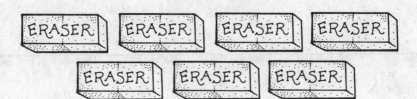

4	5	6	7
○	○	○	○

Spiral Review

2

3

2

DIRECTIONS **1.** Count and tell how many erasers. Mark under your answer. **(Lesson 3.4)** **2.** Which set has the same number of objects as the cube train? Mark under your answer. **(Lesson 1.3)** **3.** Which set shows the number? Mark under your answer. **(Lesson 1.2)**

Name _____

Model 8

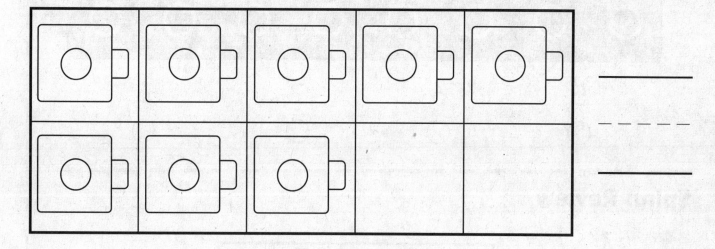

8 is ___ less than 10

DIRECTIONS 1. Place cubes on the ones in the ten frame. Tell how many cubes. Write the number. 2. How many less than 10 is 8? Write the number. 3. Which sets show 8 apples? Circle those sets.

Lesson Check

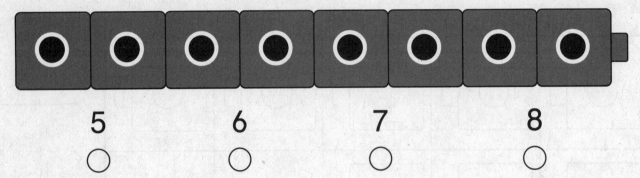

5   6   7   8

○   ○   ○   ○

Spiral Review

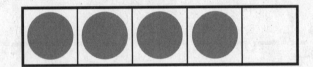

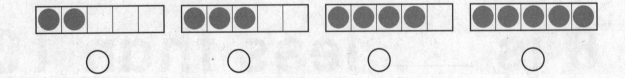

○   ○   ○   ○

one   two   three   four

○   ○   ○   ○

DIRECTIONS **1.** How many cubes? Mark under your answer.
(Lesson 3.5) **2.** Count and tell how many counters are in the five frame. Which
set has more counters? Mark under your answer. **(Lesson 2.4)** **3.** Count
and tell how many stop signs. Mark under your answer. **(Lesson 1.1)**

Read and Write 8

1

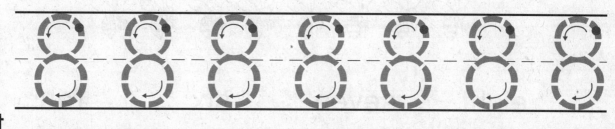

8
eight

2

_____

- - - - - - - - - - - - -

_____

3

_____

- - - - - - - - - - - - -

_____

4

_____

- - - - - - - - - - - - -

_____

5

_____

- - - - - - - - - - - - -

_____

DIRECTIONS **1.** Say the number. Trace the numbers.
2–5. Count and tell how many. Write the number.

Lesson Check

1

eight	seven	six	four
◯	◯	◯	◯

Spiral Review

2

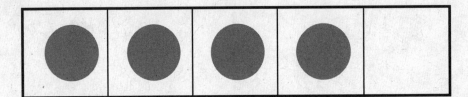

| ◯ | ◯ | ◯ | ◯ |

3

2	3	4	5
◯	◯	◯	◯

DIRECTIONS 1. Count and tell how many bees. Mark under your answer.
(Lesson 3.6) 2. Count and tell how many counters are in the five frame.
Which set of crickets has one more than the counters? Mark under your answer.
(Lesson 2.2) 3. Count and tell how many beetles. Mark under your answer. **(Lesson 1.6)**

Model 9

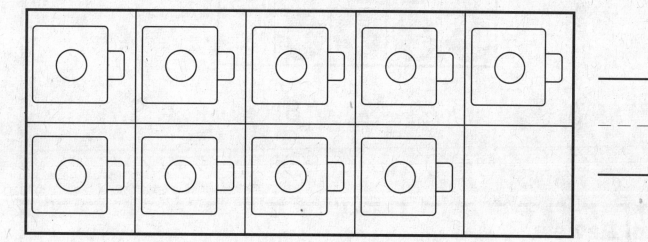

_____
_ _ _ _ _
_____

9 is ___ less than 10

DIRECTIONS **1.** Place cubes on the ones in the ten frame. Tell how many cubes. Write the number. **2.** How many less than 10 is 9? Write the number. **3.** Which sets show 9 stars? Circle those sets.

Chapter 3

Lesson Check

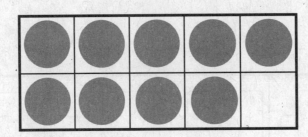

6　　　7　　　8　　　9

◯　　　◯　　　◯　　　◯

Spiral Review

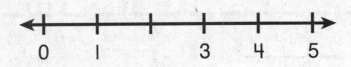

1　　　2　　　3　　　4

◯　　　◯　　　◯　　　◯

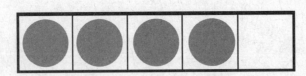

1　　　2　　　3　　　4

◯　　　◯　　　◯　　　◯

DIRECTIONS **1.** How many counters? Mark under your answer.
(Lesson 3.7) **2.** What number is missing on the number line? Mark under your
answer. (Lesson 2.6) **3.** How many counters? Mark under your answer.
(Lesson 1.4)

Name _____

Read and Write 9

9
nine

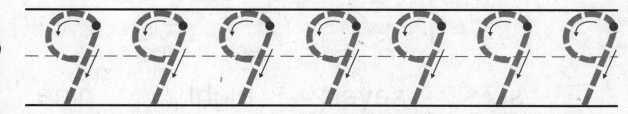

2

_____

‒ ‒ ‒ ‒ ‒ ‒ ‒

_____

3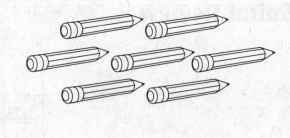

_____

‒ ‒ ‒ ‒ ‒ ‒ ‒

_____

4

_____

‒ ‒ ‒ ‒ ‒ ‒ ‒

_____

5

_____

‒ ‒ ‒ ‒ ‒ ‒ ‒

_____

DIRECTIONS **1.** Say the number. Trace the numbers.
2–5. Count and tell how many. Write the number.

Lesson Check

1

six   seven   eight   nine
○   ○   ○   ○

Spiral Review

2

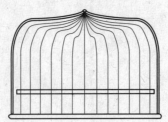

0   1   2   3
○   ○   ○   ○

3

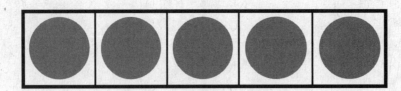

2   3   4   5
○   ○   ○   ○

DIRECTIONS 1. Count and tell how many squirrels. Mark under your answer.
(Lesson 3.8)   2. How many birds are in the cage? Mark under your answer.
(Lesson 1.8)   3. How many counters? Mark under your answer. (Lesson 1.6)

P56 fifty-six

Model 10

1

_____

- - - - - - -   Y   - - - - - - -   R

_____

2

_____

- - - - - - -   Y   - - - - - - -   R

_____

DIRECTIONS   1–2. Spill ten two-color counters on the page. Sort counters by color. Place the counters in the ten frame by Y - yellow color or R - red color. Draw the counters in the ten frame. Write how many of each color.

Lesson Check

1

10	9	7	5
○	○	○	○

Spiral Review

2

○   ○   ○   ○

3

one	two	three	four
○	○	○	○

DIRECTIONS **1.** Count and tell how many umbrellas. Mark under your answer. (Lesson 3.9) **2.** Which set of counters shows the same number as the kites. Mark under your answer. (Lesson 2.1) **3.** Count and tell how many raincoats. Mark under your answer. (Lesson 1.2)

P58 fifty-eight

Name _____

Read and Write 10

1

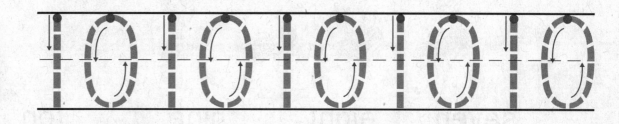

10
ten

2

_____

- - - - - - - - - - - -

_____

3

_____

- - - - - - - - - - - -

_____

4

_____

- - - - - - - - - - - -

_____

DIRECTIONS 1. Say the number. Trace the numbers.
2–4. Count and tell how many. Write the number.

Chapter 3

Lesson Check

seven   eight   nine   ten

◯   ◯   ◯   ◯

Spiral Review

◯   ◯   ◯   ◯

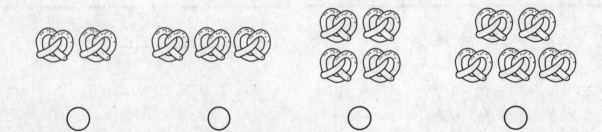

◯   ◯   ◯   ◯

DIRECTIONS   **1.** Count and tell how many ears of corn. Mark under your answer. **(Lesson 3.10)**   **2.** Count and tell how many bananas. Which set has fewer counters than bananas? Mark under your answer.   **(Lesson 2.3)**   **3.** Which set has 5 pretzels? Mark under your answer.   **(Lesson 1.5)**

Name _____

Hands On: How Many Ones?

 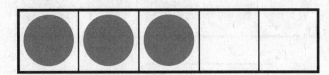

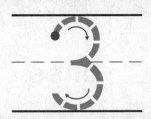

3 _____ ones

· ·

 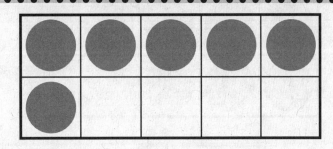

_____

_ _ _ _ _ _ _

_____ ones

· ·

 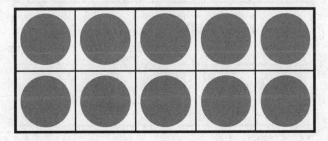

_____   _____

_ _ _ _ _   OR   _ _ _ _ _

_____ ones   _____ ten

DIRECTIONS   Place counters on the ones shown.   **1.** How many counters? How many ones is that? Trace the number.   **2.** How many counters? How many ones is that? Write the number.   **3.** How many counters? How many ones is that? How many tens is that?

Chapter 3   sixty **P60a**

4

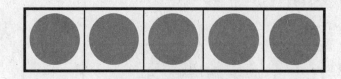

_____

- - - - - - - -

_____ **ones**

5

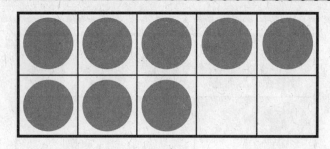

_____

- - - - - - - -

_____ **ones**

6

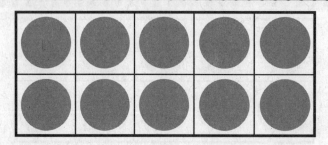

_____   _____

- - - - - - -   **OR**   - - - - - - -

_____ **ones**   _____ **ten**

DIRECTIONS Place counters on the ones shown. **4–5.** How many counters?
How many ones is that? Write the number. **6.** How many counters? How many
ones is that? How many tens is that?

P60b sixty

Ways to Make 10

cubes

cubes

cubes

7

9

8

1

2

3

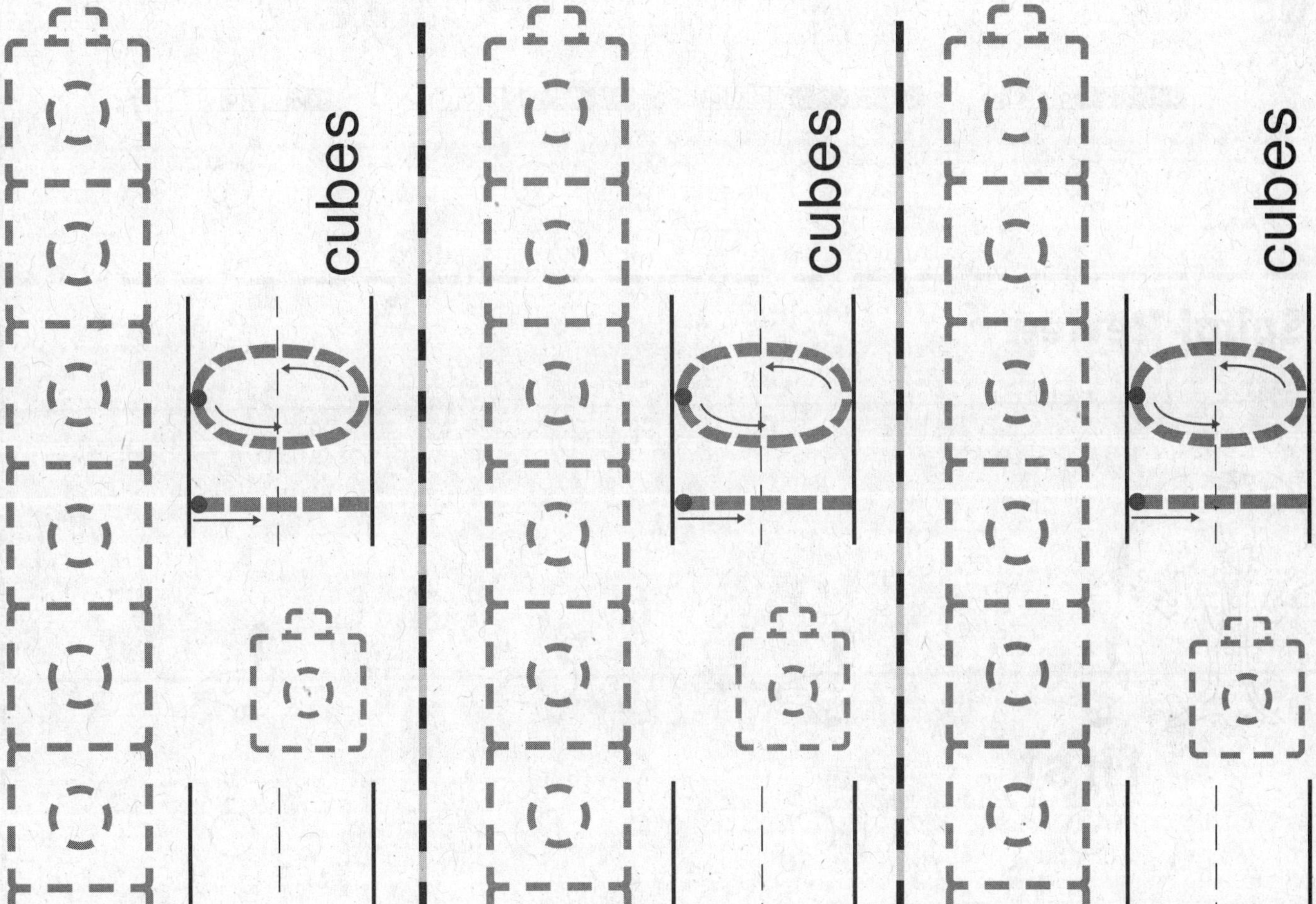

DIRECTIONS 1–3. Use blue to color the cubes to match the number. Use red to color the other cubes. Write how many red cubes. Trace the number that shows how many cubes in all.

Lesson Check

 ○ ○ ○ ○

Spiral Review

first

○ ○ ○ ○

| 1 | 2 | 3 | 4 |

○ ○ ○ ○

DIRECTIONS 1. Which cube train shows a way to make 10? Mark under your answer. (Lesson 3.11) 2. Which goose is third from the tree? Mark under your answer. (Lesson 2.7) 3. How many birds? Mark under your answer. (Lesson 1.4)

Name _____

Make a Model • Compare Numbers to 10

_____

- - - - - - -

_____

- - - - - - -

_____

_____

_____

- - - - - - -

_____

_____

- - - - - - -

_____

DIRECTIONS **1.** There are 7 red balloons and 4 fewer blue balloons. Use cube trains to model the sets of balloons. Draw and color the cube trains. Write how many. Which number is less? Circle that number. **2.** There are 8 red balloons and 3 fewer blue balloons. Use cube trains to model the sets of balloons. Draw and color the cube trains. Write how many. Which number is greater? Circle that number.

Lesson Check

1	2	3	4
○	○	○	○

Spiral Review

○	○	○	○

○	○	○	○

DIRECTIONS **1.** How many fewer cubes are in the bottom cube train? Mark under your answer. **(Lesson 3.12)** **2.** Which picture shows more balls than kites? Mark under your answer. **(Lesson 2.2)** **3.** Which set shows the number? Mark under your answer. **(Lesson 1.6)**

© Houghton Mifflin Harcourt Publishing Company

Name _____

Count Forward to 10

1

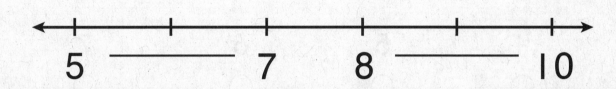

2

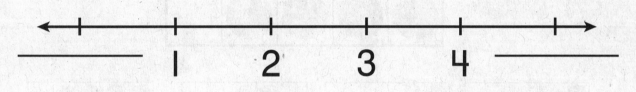

3

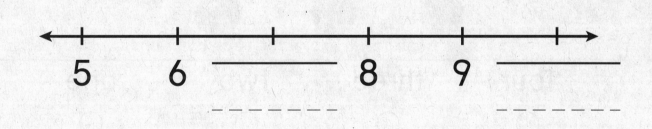

DIRECTIONS 1. Begin with 5. Count forward. Write the missing numbers. **2.** Begin with 0. Count forward. Write the missing numbers. **3.** Begin with 5. Count forward. Write the missing numbers.

Chapter 3

Lesson Check

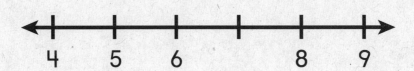

4	5	6	7
○	○	○	○

Spiral Review

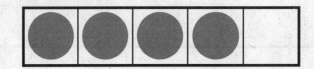

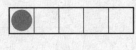   

four	three	two	one
○	○	○	○

DIRECTIONS 1. Begin with 4. Count forward. What is the missing number? Mark under your answer. (Lesson 3.13) 2. Count and tell how many counters are in the five frame. Mark under the set of counters that has one fewer counter. (Lesson 2.3) 3. How many counters? Mark under your answer. (Lesson 1.4)

P66 sixty-six

Count Backward from 10

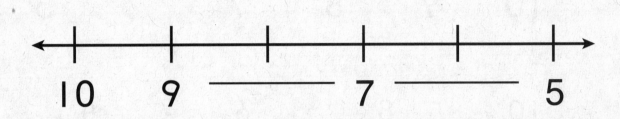

①

10   9   ____   7   ____   5

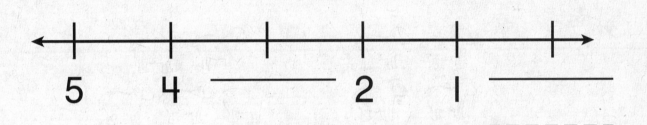

②

5   4   ____   2   1   ____

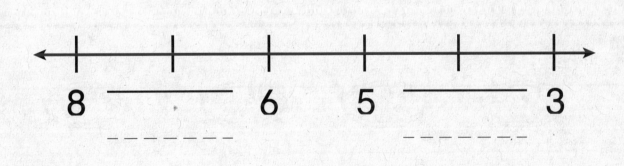

③

8   ____   6   5   ____   3

DIRECTIONS 1. Begin with 10. Count backward. Write the missing numbers. **2.** Begin with 5. Count backward. Write the missing numbers. **3.** Begin with 8. Count backward. Write the missing numbers.

1

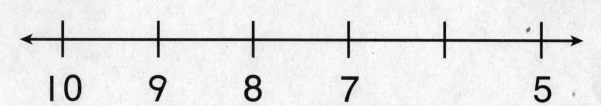

10   9   8   7   5

10   8   6   4
○   ○   ○   ○

Spiral Review

2

3   4   5   6
○   ○   ○   ○

3

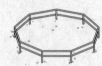

○   ○   ○   ○

DIRECTIONS   1. Begin with 10. Count backward. What is the missing number. Mark under your answer. **(Lesson 3.14)   2.** Look at the two groups of sheep. How many sheep are in the group that has more? Mark under your answer. **(Lesson 2.4)   3.** Which pen has 0 sheep in it? Mark under your answer. **(Lesson 1.7)**

Chapter 3 Extra Practice

Lessons 3.1 – 3.6 (pp. 89 – 112)

six

 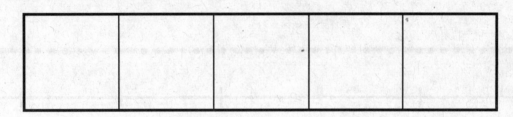

seven

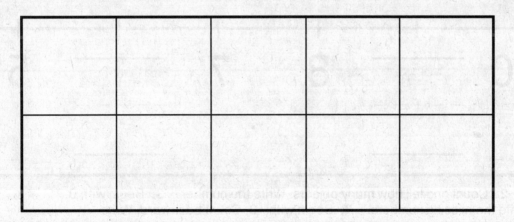

eight

DIRECTIONS **I–3.** Use cubes to show the number. Draw the cubes. Trace the number.

1

_____

- - - - - - - - - - -

_____

2

_____

- - - - - - - - - - -

_____

3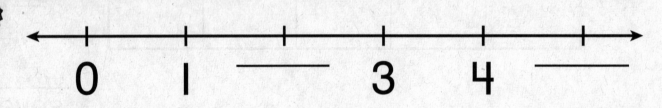

0   1   ____   3   4   ____

      - - - -   - - - -

      ____   ____

4

10   ____   8   7   ____   5

       - - - -   - - - -

       ____   ____

DIRECTIONS 1–2. Count and tell how many objects. Write the number. 3. Begin with 0. Count forward. Write the missing numbers. 4. Begin with 10. Count backward. Write the missing numbers.

© Houghton Mifflin Harcourt Publishing Company

School-Home Letter

Dear Family,

My class started Chapter 4 today. In this chapter, I will learn all about addition and subtraction. I will also learn how to tell an addition and subtraction story.

Love, _____

Vocabulary

plus (+) a symbol that shows addition

plus
↓
$3 + 2 = 5$

minus (−) a symbol that shows subtraction

minus
↓
$3 - 2 = 1$

Home Activity

Invite your child to act out addition and subtraction stories. For example, your child can show you 4 socks, add 2 more socks, and then tell you the addition sentence.

$4 + 2 = 6$

Find other objects that can be used to act out a subtraction story.

Literature

Look for these books at the library. You and your child will enjoy these interactive books that will strengthen addition and subtraction skills.

Math Stories: Addition by Rosemary Shannon. Kids Can Press, 2003.

Elevator Magic by Stuart J. Murphy. HarperTrophy, 1997.

Carta
para la casa

Querida familia:

Mi clase comenzó hoy el Capítulo 4. En este capítulo, aprenderé todo sobre la suma y la resta. También aprenderé cómo contar un cuento de suma y resta.

Con cariño, _____

Vocabulario

más (+) signo que indica suma

signo de suma
↓
$3 + 2 = 5$

menos (−) signo que indica resta

signo de resta
↓
$3 - 2 = 1$

Actividad para la casa

Anime a su hijo a representar cuentos de suma y de resta. Por ejemplo, puede mostrar 4 calcetines, agregar 2 calcetines más, y luego decir el enunciado de suma.

$$4 + 2 = 6$$

Busquen otros objetos que puedan usarse para representar cuentos de resta.

Literatura

Busquen estos libros en la biblioteca. Usted y su hijo disfrutarán estos libros interactivos que sirven para reforzar las destrezas de suma y resta.

Math Stories: Addition
por Rosemary Shannon. Kids Can Press, 2003.

El ascensor maravilloso
por Stuart J. Murphy. HarperTrophy, 1997.

Name _____

Act It Out • Joining Problems

_____
- - - - - - - -
_____

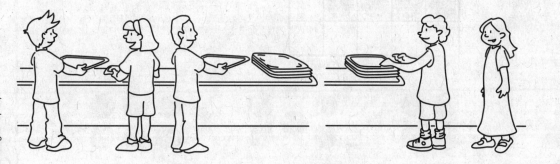

_____
- - - - - - - -
_____

DIRECTIONS 1–2. Tell a joining story problem.
Write the number that shows how many children in all.

Chapter 4

seventy-three **P73**

Lesson Check

1

7	8	9	10
○	○	○	○

Spiral Review

2

four	five	six	seven
○	○	○	○

3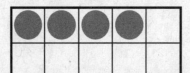

DIRECTIONS **1.** How many cats in all? Mark under your answer. **(Lesson 4.1)**
2. Count and tell how many tigers. Mark under your answer. **(Lesson 3.2)** **3.** Count and tell how many counters are in the ten frame. Mark under the set of counters that shows the same number of counters. **(Lesson 2.1)**

Name _____

Algebra: Model Joining

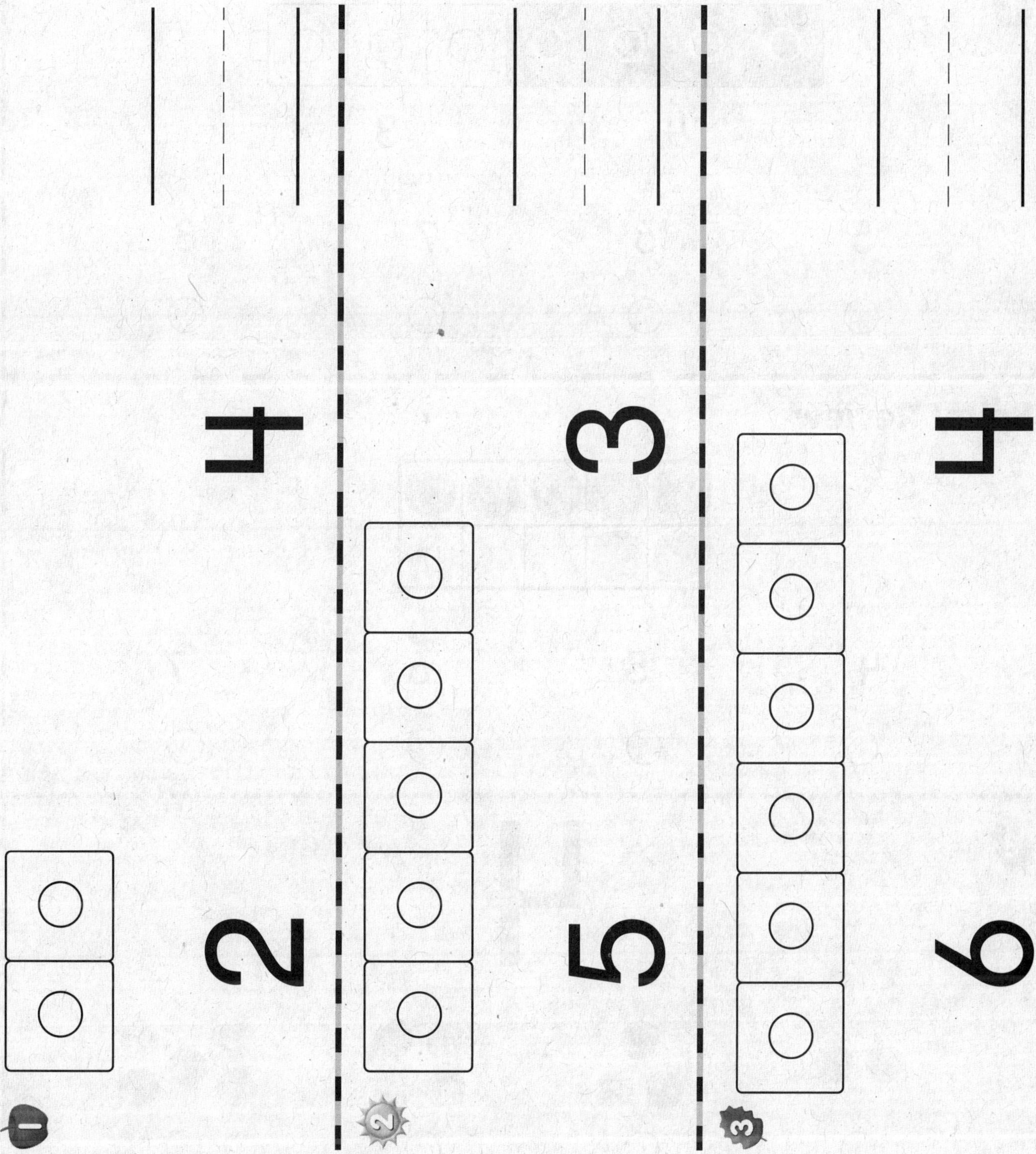

4

3

4

1 **2**

2 **5**

3 **6**

DIRECTIONS 1–3. Tell a joining story problem.
Model the story problem with cubes. Draw and
color the cubes that are joining the set. Write the
number that shows how many in all.

Chapter 4

Lesson Check

1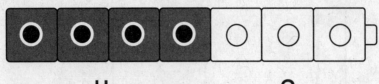

4   3

5   6   7   8
○   ○   ○   ○

Spiral Review

2

4   5   6   7
○   ○   ○   ○

3

4

                              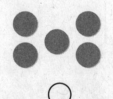

○   ○   ○   ○

DIRECTIONS   1. How many cubes in all? Mark under your
answer. **(Lesson 4.2)   2.** How many counters? Mark under your
answer. **(Lesson 3.3)   3.** Which set shows the number? **(Lesson 1.4)**

P76 seventy-six

Name _____

Algebra: Join Sets

 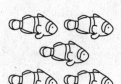   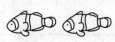

_____   _____   _____

- - - - - - - - **and** - - - - - - - - **is** - - - - - - - -

_____   _____   _____

_____   _____   _____

- - - - - - - - **and** - - - - - - - - **is** - - - - - - - -

_____   _____   _____

_____   _____   _____

- - - - - - - - **and** - - - - - - - - **is** - - - - - - - -

_____   _____   _____

DIRECTIONS 1–3. Tell a joining story problem about the sets.
Write how many in each set. Circle the two sets to join them. Write
how many in all.

Lesson Check

1

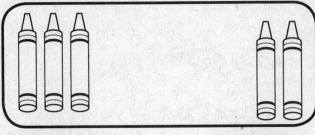

3 and **2** is _____

   4   5   6   7
   ○   ○   ○   ○

Spiral Review

2

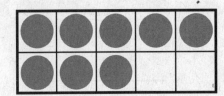

8 is _____ less than 10

   1   2   3   4
   ○   ○   ○   ○

3

   1   2   3   4
   ○   ○   ○   ○

DIRECTIONS 1. How many crayons in all? Mark under your answer. **(Lesson 4.3)** 2. 8 is how many less than 10? Mark under your answer. **(Lesson 3.5)** 3. How many paintbrushes? Mark under your answer. **(Lesson 1.4)**

Name _____

Algebra: Introduce Symbols to Add

3   **plus**   **5**   **is**   **8**

___    (plus sign)   ___   = (equals)   ___

___

 ❷

6   **plus**   **4**   **is**   **10**

___   (plus sign)   ___   = (equals)   ___

___

---

❸

7   **plus**   **2**   **is**   **9**

___   (plus sign)   ___   = (equals)   ___

___

DIRECTIONS   **1–3.** Tell a joining story problem. Write how many in each set. Circle the two sets to join them. Trace the symbols. Write how many in all.

 © Houghton Mifflin Harcourt Publishing Company

Chapter 4   seventy-nine **P79**

Lesson Check

3   plus   4   is

$$3 + 4 =$$ _____

4	5	6	7
○	○	○	○

Spiral Review

4	5	6	7
○	○	○	○

   ○   ○   ○   ○

DIRECTIONS   **1.** How many trucks in all? Mark under your answer. **(Lesson 4.4)**   **2.** How many cars? Mark under your answer. **(Lesson 3.4)**   **3.** Count and tell how many bikes. Mark under the set of counters that shows fewer. **(Lesson 2.5)**

Addition Expressions

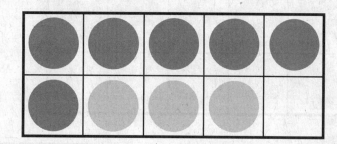

more than

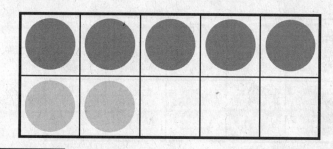

_____ _____

_____ more than _____

_____ + _____

DIRECTIONS 1. Look at the dark counters in the ten frame. How many light counters are being added? Trace the numbers in the statement to show how many more. Trace to complete the expression. 2. Look at the dark counters in the ten frame. How many light counters are being added? Write the numbers in the statement to show how many more. Write to complete the expression.

Chapter 4

eighty **P80a**

3

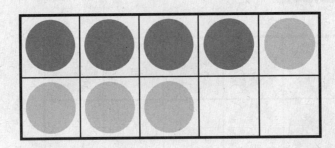

_____   _____

_ _ _ _ _   _ _ _ _ _

_____   **more than**   _____

_ _ _ _ _   _ _ _ _ _

_____   _____

· ·

4

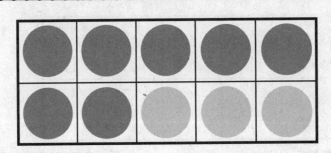

_____   _____

_ _ _ _ _   _ _ _ _ _

_____   **more than**   _____

_____   _____

_ _ _ _ _   _ _ _ _ _

_____   _____

DIRECTIONS   3–4. Look at the dark counters in the ten frame.
How many light counters are being added? Write the numbers in the
statement to show how many more. Write to complete the expression.

P80b eighty

Algebra: Addition Sentences

1

_____   _____   _____

_ _ _ _   **+**   _ _ _ _   **=**   _ _ _ _

_____   _____   _____

2

_____   _____   _____

_ _ _ _   **+**   _ _ _ _   **=**   _ _ _ _

_____   _____   _____

3

_____   _____   _____

_ _ _ _   **+**   _ _ _ _   **=**   _ _ _ _

_____   _____   _____

4

_____   _____   _____

_ _ _ _   **+**   _ _ _ _   **=**   _ _ _ _

_____   _____   _____

DIRECTIONS   1–4. Tell a joining story problem.
Complete the addition sentence to show how many in all.

Lesson Check

1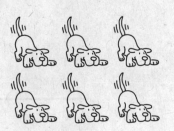

$$6 + 3 = \text{------}$$

7	8	9	10
○	○	○	○

Spiral Review

2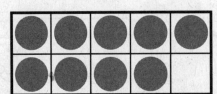

9 is ___ less than 10

1	2	3	4
○	○	○	○

3

2	3	4	5
○	○	○	○

DIRECTIONS **1.** Mark under your answer to show how many in all. **(Lesson 4.5)**
2. 9 is how many less than 10? Mark under your answer. **(Lesson 3.7)**   **3.** Count and tell how many. Mark under your answer. **(Lesson 1.6)**

Name _____

Algebra: Break Apart a Set

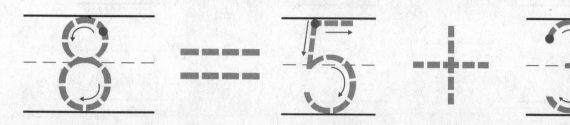

$$8 = 5 + 3$$

$$\_\_ = \_\_ + \_\_$$

$$\_\_ = \_\_ + \_\_$$

DIRECTIONS **I.** Look at the cube train. Trace the numbers that complete the equation. **2–3.** Write to complete the equation.

Chapter 4

4

_____ === _____ + _____

5

_____ === _____ + _____

6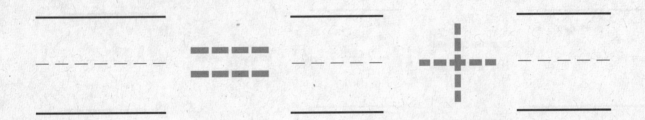

_____ === _____ + _____

DIRECTIONS 4–6. Write to complete the equation.

P82b eighty-two

Name _____

Algebra: Add Equal Sets

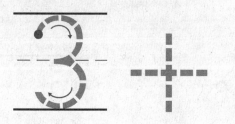 

 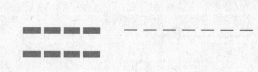

DIRECTIONS 1–2. Create a cube train with the same number of cubes as the cube train shown. Draw and color the cube train. Tell a joining story problem. Complete the addition sentence.

Lesson Check

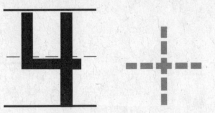 

4	6	8	10
◯	◯	◯	◯

Spiral Review

first

◯　　◯　　◯　　◯　　◯

0	1	2	3
◯	◯	◯	◯

DIRECTIONS 1. Mark under the number to complete the addition sentence. **(Lesson 4.6)**
2. Which turtle is third in line? Mark under your answer. **(Lesson 2.7)** 3. How many fish are in the bowl? Mark under your answer. **(Lesson 1.8)**

Algebra: Create and Model Addition Problems

_____ + _____ == _____

- -

_____ + _____ == _____

© Houghton Mifflin Harcourt Publishing Company

DIRECTIONS 1–2. Create an addition story problem. Model your story with counters. Draw and color the counters. Complete the addition sentence to show how many in all. Tell your addition story problem.

Chapter 4

Lesson Check

$$3 + 4 = 7$$

○   ○   ○   ○

Spiral Review

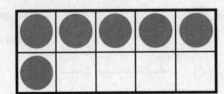

three   four   five   six

four   three   two   one

○   ○   ○   ○

DIRECTIONS 1. Mark under the model that shows how many in all.
(Lesson 4.7) 2. How many counters? Mark under your answer.
(Lesson 3.2) 3. How many erasers? Mark under your answer. (Lesson 1.2)

Name _____

Act It Out • Separating Problems

DIRECTIONS Tell a separating story problem. **1.** Write the number that shows how many birds are left. **2.** Write the number that shows how many beavers are left.

Chapter 4

eighty-seven **P87**

Lesson Check

1	2	3	4
○	○	○	○

Spiral Review

7	8	9	10
○	○	○	○

DIRECTIONS **1.** What number shows how many are left? Mark under your answer. **(Lesson 4.8)** **2.** Count and tell how many. Mark under your answer. **(Lesson 3.8)** **3.** Count and tell how many counters are in the five frame. Mark under the set of counters that shows one more counter. **(Lesson 2.2)**

Name _____

Algebra: Model Separating

1

[empty box]

$$5 \qquad 4 \qquad \underline{}$$

- -

2

[empty box]

$$8 \qquad 3 \qquad \underline{}$$

DIRECTIONS 1–2. Tell a separating story problem. Model the story with cubes. Write the number that shows how many are left. Draw to show how you solved the problem.

Lesson Check

1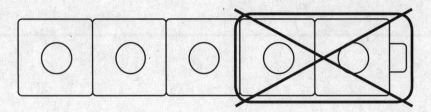

2 3 4 5
○ ○ ○ ○

Spiral Review

2

3 4 5 6
○ ○ ○ ○

3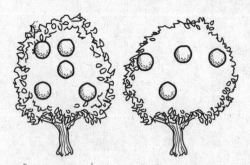

4 5 6 7
○ ○ ○ ○

DIRECTIONS 1. How many cubes are left? Mark under your answer. (Lesson 4.9) 2. Begin with 5. Count forward. What is the missing number? Mark under your answer. (Lesson 3.13) 3. Compare the sets of apples. How many apples are in the tree that has more? Mark under your answer. (Lesson 2.4)

P90 ninety

Name _____

Algebra: Separate Sets

_____   take away **3** is   _____
- - - - -   - - - - -
_____   _____

_____   take away **4** is   _____
- - - - -   - - - - -
_____   _____

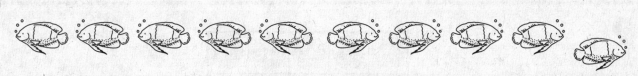

_____   take away **5** is   _____
- - - - -   - - - - -
_____   _____

DIRECTIONS 1–3. Tell a separating story problem. Write how many there are in all. Circle the set that you take away. Mark an X on that set. Write how many are left.

Chapter 4

Lesson Check

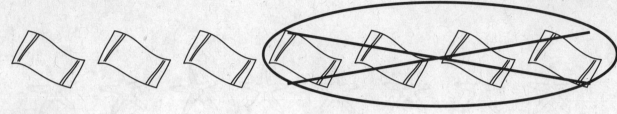

7   take away   4   is   _____

3   4   5   6
○   ○   ○   ○

Spiral Review

    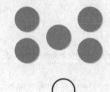

○   ○   ○   ○

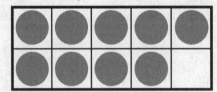

7   8   9   10
○   ○   ○   ○

DIRECTIONS 1. How many beach towels are left? Mark under your answer.
(Lesson 4.10) 2. Count and tell how many umbrellas. Mark under the set of counters
that shows one more. (Lesson 2.2) 3. How many counters? Mark under your answer.
(Lesson 3.7)

Name _____

Algebra: Introduce Symbols to Subtract

1

10	minus	4	is	6

_____   ---- -   _ _ _ _ _ _ _   ≡≡≡   _ _ _ _ _ _

_____   _____   _____

2

7	minus	5	is	2

_____   ---- -   _ _ _ _ _ _ _   ≡≡≡   _ _ _ _ _ _

_____   _____   _____

3

9	minus	3	is	6

_____   ---- -   _ _ _ _ _ _ _   ≡≡≡   _ _ _ _ _ _

_____   _____   _____

DIRECTIONS 1–3. Tell a separating story problem. Write how many birds there are in all. Circle the set that you take away. Mark an X on that set. Trace the symbols. Complete the subtraction sentence.

Chapter 4

Lesson Check

1

5   minus   3   is

 5 ---- 3 === _____

1   2   3   4
○   ○   ○   ○

Spiral Review

2

7   8   9   10
○   ○   ○   ○

3

○   ○   ○   ○

DIRECTIONS **1.** How many boats are left? Mark under your answer.
(Lesson 4.11) **2.** How many sunglasses? Mark under your answer. (Lesson 3.6)
3. Count and tell how many teddy bears. Mark under the set of counters that
shows the same number. (Lesson 2.1)

Subtraction Expressions

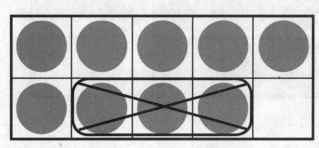

 take away

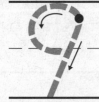 —

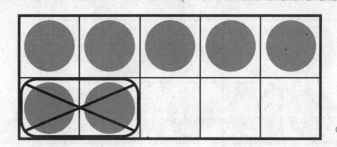

_____   take away   _____

_____   —   _____

DIRECTIONS **I.** Look at the counters in the ten frame. How many counters are being taken away? Trace the numbers in the statement. Trace to complete the expression. **2.** Look at the counters in the ten frame. How many counters are being taken away? Write the numbers in the statement. Write to complete the expression.

Chapter 4

3

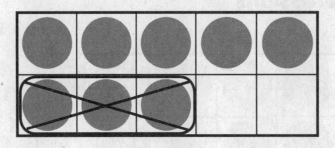

_____   _____

take away

_____   _____

= = =

_____   _____

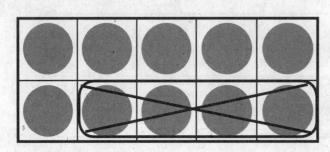

_____   _____

take away

_____   _____

= = =

_____   _____

DIRECTIONS **3–4.** Look at the counters in the ten frame. How many counters are being taken away? Write the numbers in the statement. Write to complete the expression.

Equal To

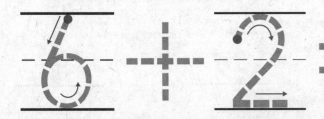 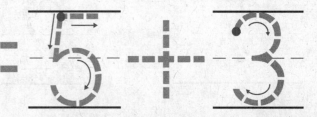

6 + 2 = 5 + 3

___ + ___ = ___ + ___

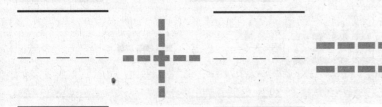

___ + ___ = ___ + ___

DIRECTIONS Look at the cube trains. **1.** Trace to complete the equation. **2–3.** Write to complete the equation.

Chapter 4

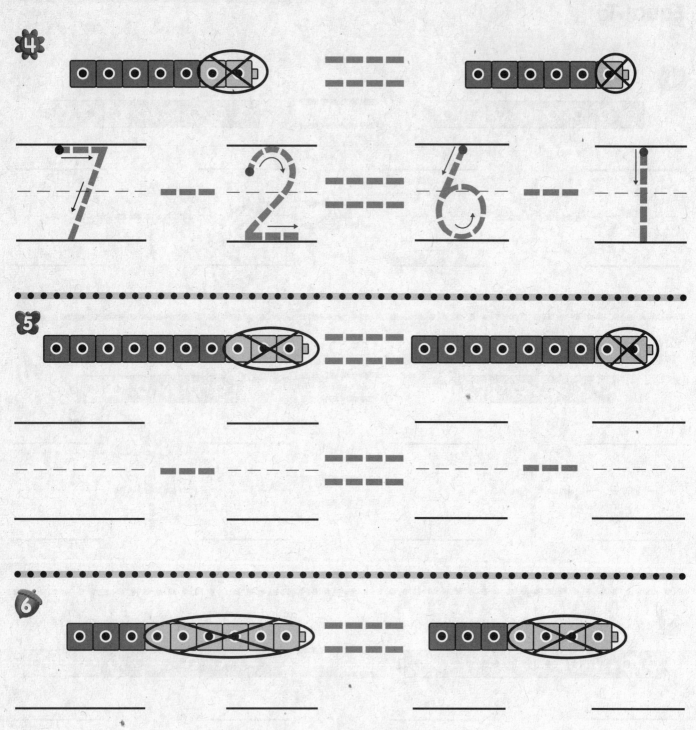

4.

$7 - 2 = 6 - 1$

5.

6.

DIRECTIONS Look at the cube trains. **4.** Trace to complete the equation. **5–6.** Write to complete the equation.

P94d ninety-four

Algebra: Subtraction Sentences

1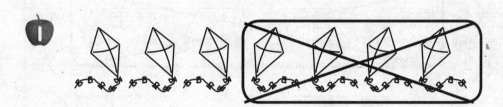

_____   ▭▭   _____   ▭▭▭   _____
                                          ▭▭▭

_____   _____

2

_____   ▭▭   _____   ▭▭▭▭▭   _____
                                  ▭▭▭

_____   _____

3

_____   _____

_____   ▭▭   _____   ▭▭▭   _____
                                  ▭▭▭

_____   _____

DIRECTIONS   **1–3.** Tell a separating story problem about the toys. Complete the subtraction sentence to show how many are left.

Lesson Check

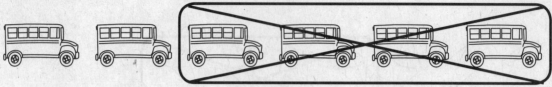

6 --- 4 === ___

1   2   3   4

○   ○   ○   ○

Spiral Review

4   5   6   7

○   ○   ○   ○

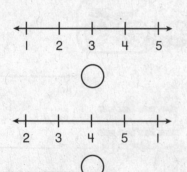

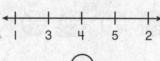

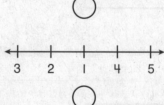

DIRECTIONS 1. Mark under your answer to show how many are left.
(Lesson 4.12) 2. How many lunch boxes? Mark under your answer.
(Lesson 3.4) 3. Which number line shows the numbers in the correct order?
Mark under your answer. (Lesson 2.6)

Algebra: Create and Model Subtraction Problems

1

2

DIRECTIONS **1–2.** Create a subtraction story problem. Model your story with counters. Draw the counters. Circle the set that you take away. Mark an X on that set. Complete the subtraction sentence to show how many are left.

Lesson Check

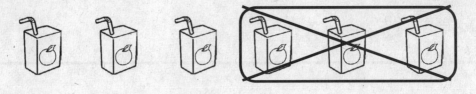

$$6 - 3 = \underline{\quad}$$

1	2	3	4
○	○	○	○

Spiral Review

2

six	seven	eight	nine
○	○	○	○

3

1	2	3	4
○	○	○	○

DIRECTIONS 1. Which number completes the subtraction sentence? Mark under your answer. (Lesson 4.13) 2. How many watermelons? Mark under your answer. (Lesson 3.8) 3. How many elephants? Mark under your answer. (Lesson 1.1)

Name _____

Algebra: Addition and Subtraction

DIRECTIONS 1–2. Tell a joining or separating word problem. Use cubes to add or subtract. Complete the number sentence.

Lesson Check

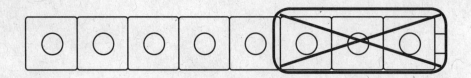

$5 + 3 = 8$ $8 - 5 = 3$ $8 - 3 = 5$ $3 + 5 = 8$

◯   ◯   ◯   ◯

Spiral Review

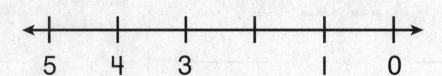

1   2   3   4

◯   ◯   ◯   ◯

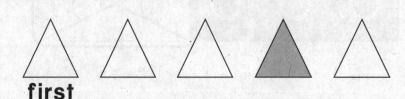

first

second   third   fourth   fifth

◯   ◯   ◯   ◯

DIRECTIONS **1.** Which number sentence matches the cubes? Mark under your answer. **(Lesson 4.14)** **2.** Begin with 5. Count backward. What is the missing number? Mark under your answer. **(Lesson 3.14)** **3.** Which triangle is shaded? Mark under your answer. **(Lesson 2.7)**

Chapter 4 Extra Practice

Lessons 4.1 – 4.7 (pp. 153–179)

1

_____
- - - - - - - - - -

2

_____
- - - - - - - - - -

3   4

_____

3

6   plus   4   is   10

____   ____   ____

\+   =

____   ____   ____

4

____   ____   ____

\+   =

____   ____   ____

DIRECTIONS **1.** Write the number that shows how many butterflies in all. **2.** Draw to show how many cubes to join. Write the number that shows how many in all. **3.** Tell a joining story problem. Write how many in each set. Circle the two sets to join them. Trace the symbols. Write how many in all. **4.** Create an addition story. Model your story with counters. Complete the addition sentence to show how many in all.

Chapter 4   one hundred one **P101**

①

_____   _____   _____

- - - - -   ▬▬   - - - - -   ▬▬▬▬   - - - - -
                              ▬▬▬

_____   _____   _____

②

_____   _____   _____   _____

- - - -   ▬▬   - - - -   ▬▬▬   - - - -
                         ▬▬▬

_____   _____   _____

③

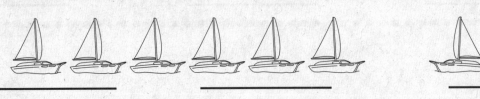

_____   _____   _____

                 ▬▬
- - - - -   ╋   - - - -   ▬▬▬   - - - - -
                 ▬▬   ▬▬▬

_____   _____   _____

DIRECTIONS   **I.** Tell a separating story problem about the cars. Complete the subtraction sentence to show how many are left.   **2.** Create a subtraction story problem. Model your story with counters. Draw the counters. Circle the set you take away. Mark an X on that set. Complete the subtraction sentence to show how many are left.   **3.** Tell a story about the picture. Circle and trace the symbol for the story. Complete the number sentence.

School-Home Letter

Dear Family,

My class started Chapter 5 today. In this chapter, I will learn how to model, read, and write the numbers 11 to 19.

Love, _____

Vocabulary

eleven a number one more than ten

sixteen a number one more than fifteen

nineteen a number one more than eighteen

Home Activity

Draw two ten frames side by side on a sheet of paper. Write a number from 11 to 19 on small sheets of paper and turn face down. Have your child draw a number from the pile and use small objects, such as pennies, to model the numbers in the ten frames.

12

Literatura

Look for this book at the library. You and your child will have fun looking at the pages while building your child's counting skills.

Counting Cranes
by Mary Beth Owens.
Little Brown, 1993.

Carta para la casa

Querida familia:

Mi clase comenzó hoy el Capítulo 5. En este capítulo, aprenderé a representar, leer y escribir los números del 11 al 19.

Con cariño, _____

Vocabulario

once uno más que diez

dieciséis uno más que quince

diecinueve uno más que dieciocho

Actividad para la casa

Dibuje dos cuadros de diez, uno al lado del otro, en una hoja de papel. Escriba un número entre 11 y 19 en pequeños trozos de papel y póngalos boca abajo. Pida a su hijo que saque un número de la pila y use objetos pequeños, como monedas de 1¢, para representar los números en los cuadros de diez.

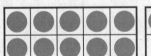 

12

Literatura

Busquen este libro en la biblioteca. Usted y su hijo se divertirán mirando las páginas mientras refuerzan las destrezas de contar.

Counting Cranes
por Mary Beth Owens.
Little Brown, 1993.

© Houghton Mifflin Harcourt Publishing Company

Model 11 and 12

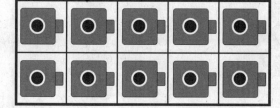 

_____

11
eleven

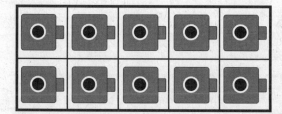 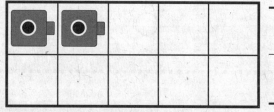

_____

12
twelve

DIRECTIONS 1. Count and tell how many. Write the number. 2. Use cubes to show 11 as one ten-cube train and some more. Draw the cubes. 3. Count and tell how many. Write the number. 4. Use cubes to show 12 as one ten-cube train and some more. Draw the cubes.

Lesson Check

Spiral Review

5   4   3   2

○   ○   ○   ○

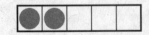         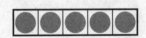

DIRECTIONS **1.** Which set has 11 objects? Mark under your answer.
(Lesson 5.1) **2.** How many ducks in all? Mark under your answer. (Lesson 4.3)
3. Count and tell how many counters are in the five frame. Mark under
the set of counters that shows one fewer counter. (Lesson 2.3)

Name _____

Build 10 and Complete the Equation

$$9 + 1 = 10$$

___ + ___ = ___

___ + ___ = ___

DIRECTIONS   1. Look at the cube train. Trace to complete the equation.   **2–3.** Look at the cube train. Write to complete the equation.

Chapter 5

one hundred six **P106a**

© Houghton Mifflin Harcourt Publishing Company

4

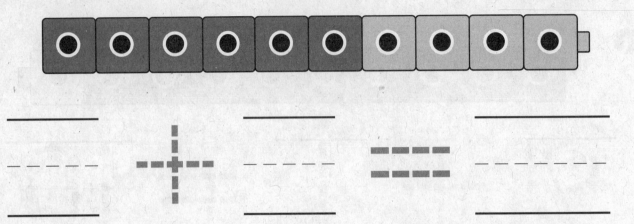

_____ + _____ = _____

5

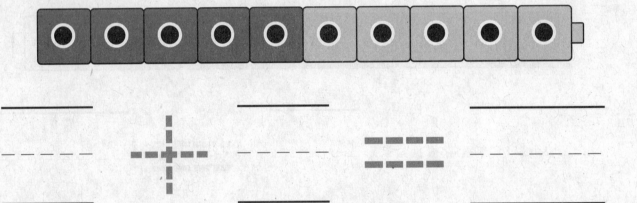

_____ + _____ = _____

6

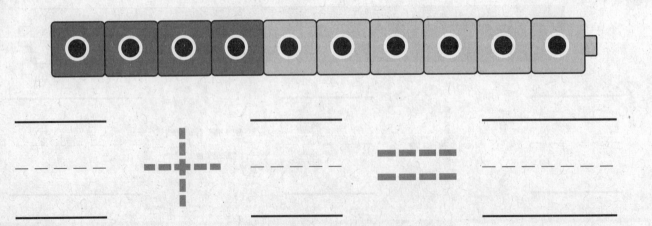

_____ + _____ = _____

DIRECTIONS   4–6. Look at the cube train. Write to complete
the equation.

P106b one hundred six

Take Apart 10 and Complete the Equation

 1

$$10 = 9 + 1$$

 2

$$10 = \underline{\quad} \quad + \quad \underline{\quad}$$

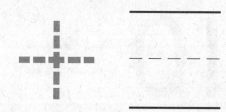

 3

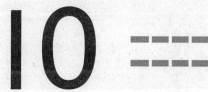

$$10 = \underline{\quad} \quad + \quad \underline{\quad}$$

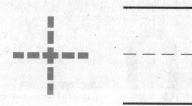

DIRECTIONS 1. Look at the cube train. Trace to complete the equation. **2–3.** Look at the cube train. Write to complete the equation.

4

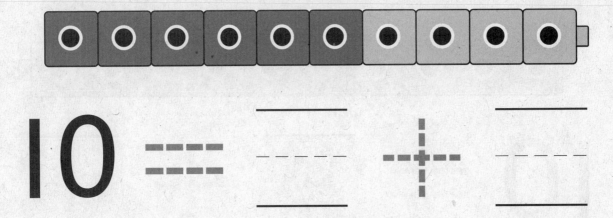

$$10 = \underline{\hspace{2cm}} + \underline{\hspace{2cm}}$$

5

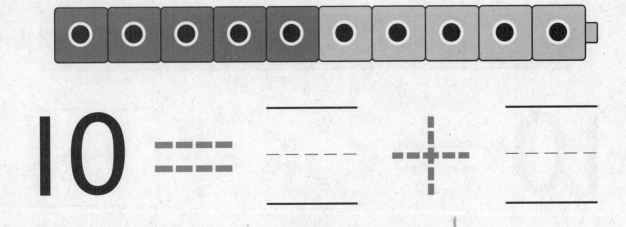

$$10 = \underline{\hspace{2cm}} + \underline{\hspace{2cm}}$$

6

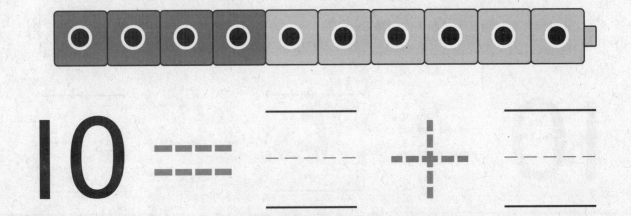

$$10 = \underline{\hspace{2cm}} + \underline{\hspace{2cm}}$$

DIRECTIONS 4–6. Look at the cube train. Write to complete the equation.

P106d one hundred six

Name _____

Read and Write 11 and 12

 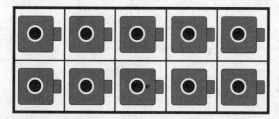 

  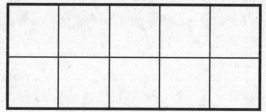

11

12

DIRECTIONS **1.** Count and tell how many cubes. Draw more cubes to show the number 11. Write the number. **2.** Count and tell how many cubes. Draw more cubes to show the number 12. Write the number. **3.** Circle a number. Draw more pumpkins to show that number.

Lesson Check

9   10   11   12

◯   ◯   ◯   ◯

Spiral Review

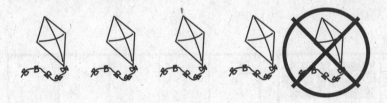

2   3   4   5

◯   ◯   ◯   ◯

1   2   3   4

◯   ◯   ◯   ◯

DIRECTIONS **1.** How many cubes? Mark under your answer.
(Lesson 5.2) **2.** Which number shows how many are left? Mark under
your answer. **(Lesson 4.10)** **3.** How many birds are in the set that has
fewer? Mark under your answer. **(Lesson 2.4)**

Read and Write 18 and 19

1

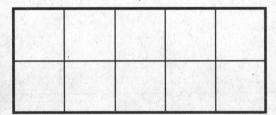

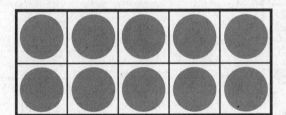 

3

17

18

19

DIRECTIONS **1.** Count and tell how many. Draw more cubes to show the number 18. Write the number. **2.** Count and tell how many. Draw more counters to show the number 19. Write the number. **3.** Circle a number. Draw more flowers to show that number.

Lesson Check

1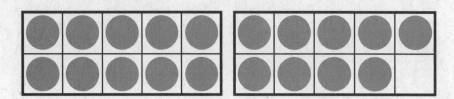

16 ○   17 ○   18 ○   19 ○

Spiral Review

2

7 ○   8 ○   9 ○   10 ○

3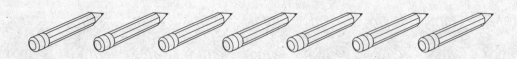

five ○   six ○   seven ○   eight ○

DIRECTIONS **1.** Count and tell how many counters. Mark under your answer. (Lesson 5.10)   **2.** Count and tell how many counters are in the ten frame. Mark under your answer. (Lesson 3.5)   **3.** How many pencils? Mark under your answer. (Lesson 3.4)

Hands On: Compare Numbers to 9 with Teen Numbers

15   8

DIRECTIONS 1. Place cubes as shown. Trace the numbers that show how many cubes. Trace the circle around the greater number. 2. Use cubes to model the numbers. Circle the greater number.

Chapter 5

one hundred twenty-four **P124a**

3

6   12

4

14   4

5

13   5

6

7   11

DIRECTIONS 3–6. Use cubes to model the numbers. Circle the
greater number.

P124b one hundred twenty-four

Compare and Order Teen Numbers

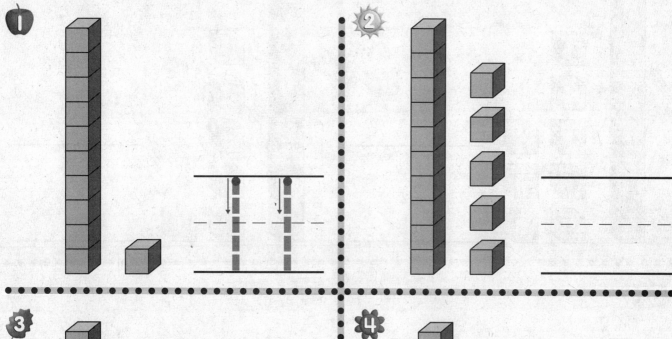

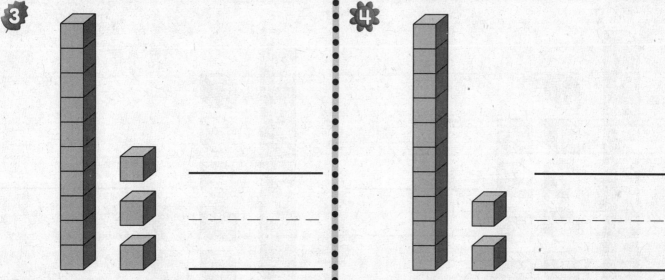

5

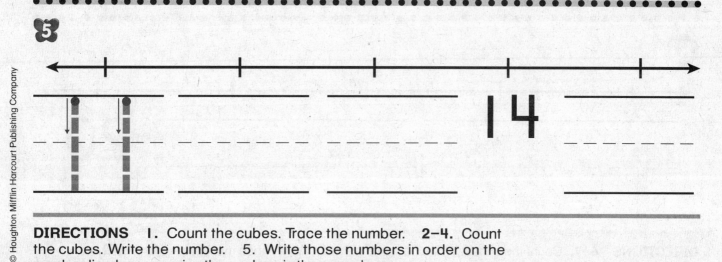

14

DIRECTIONS 1. Count the cubes. Trace the number. 2–4. Count the cubes. Write the number. 5. Write those numbers in order on the number line by comparing the numbers in the ones places.

Chapter 5

one hundred twenty-four **P124c**

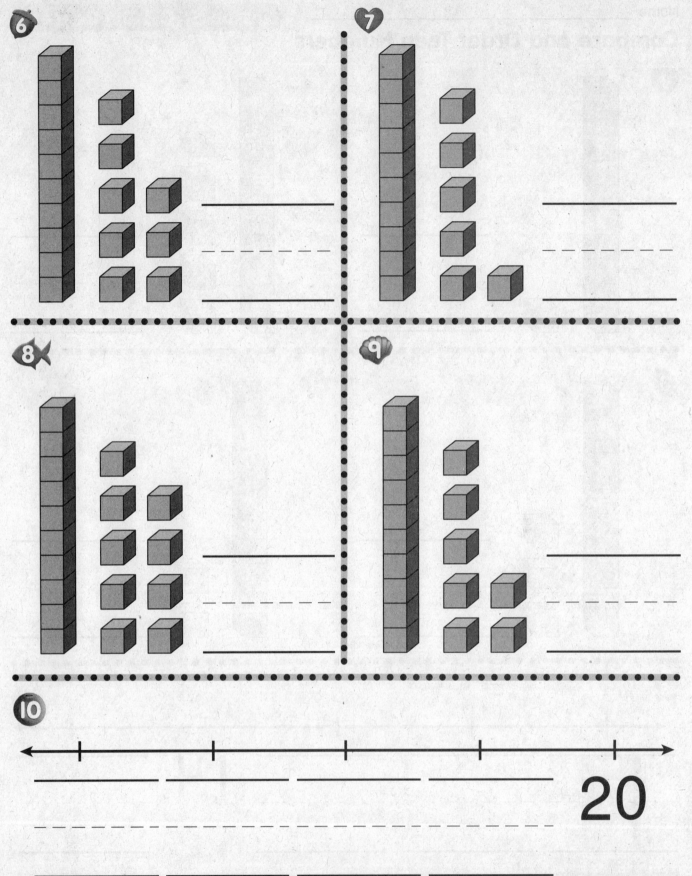

DIRECTIONS 6–9. Count the cubes. Write the number. 10. Write those numbers in order on the number line by comparing the numbers in the ones places.

P124d one hundred twenty-four

Build and Break Apart
Teen Numbers

1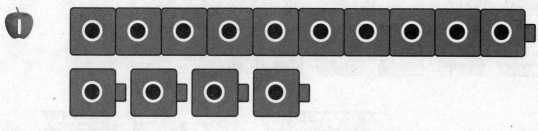

$$10 + 4 = 14$$

2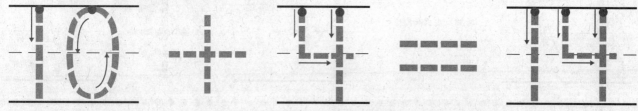

_____ + _____ = _____

3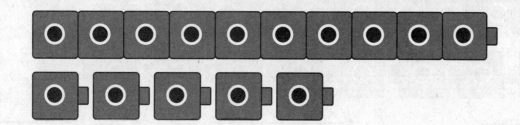

_____ + _____ = _____

DIRECTIONS **1.** Look at the cubes. Trace to complete the equation. **2–3.** Look at the cubes. Write to complete the equation.

4

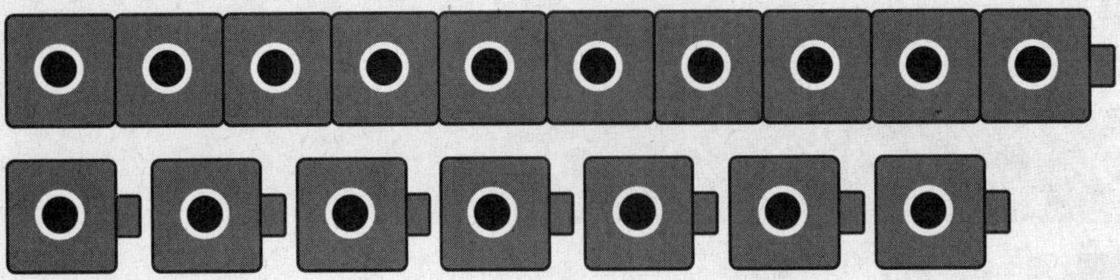

$$17 = 10 + 7$$

5

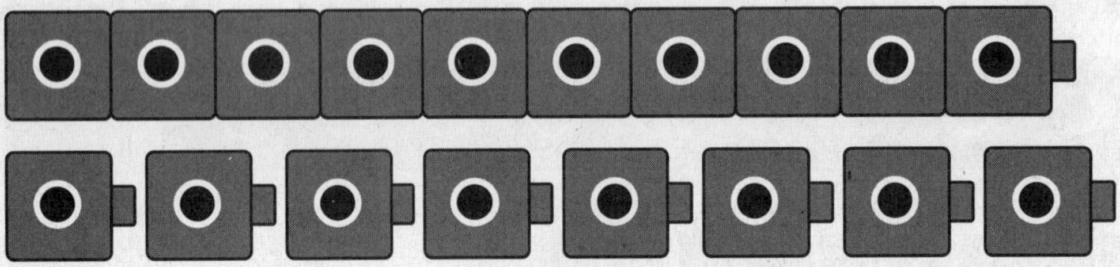

$$\underline{\qquad} = \underline{\qquad} + \underline{\qquad}$$

6

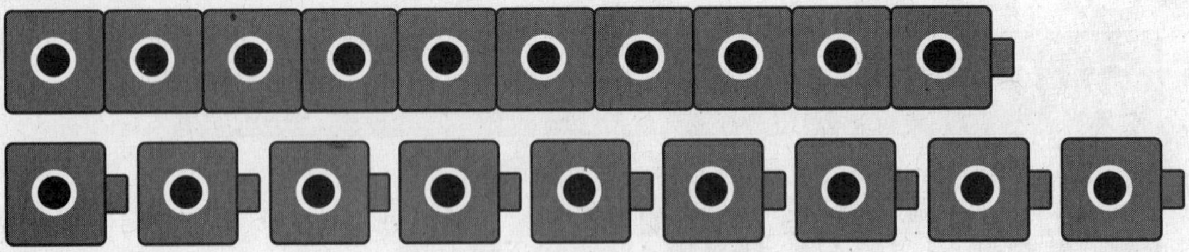

$$\underline{\qquad} = \underline{\qquad} + \underline{\qquad}$$

DIRECTIONS **4.** Look at the cubes. Trace the equation to show the teen number as one ten and some ones. **5–6.** Look at the cubes. Complete the equation to show the teen number as one ten and some ones.

P124f one hundred twenty-four

Chapter 5 Extra Practice

Lessons 5.1 – 5.4 (pp. 217 – 232)

| |

eleven

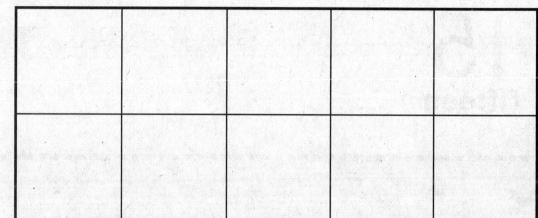

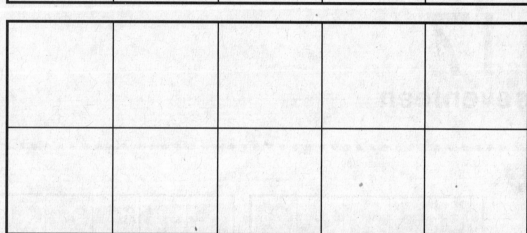

 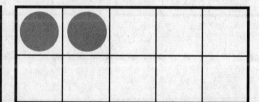

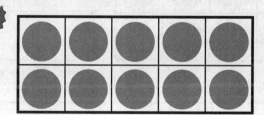

DIRECTIONS 1. Use cubes to show the number. Draw the cubes.
2–3. Count and tell how many. Write the number.

15
fifteen

17
seventeen

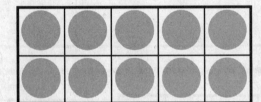 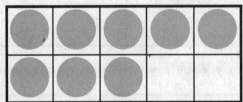

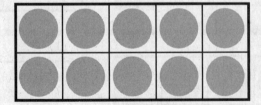 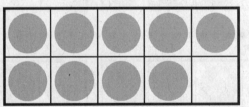

DIRECTIONS **1.** Use cubes to show 15 as one ten-cube train and some more. Draw the cubes. **2.** Use cubes to show 17 as one ten-cube train and some more. Draw the cubes. **3.** How many counters? Write the number. **4.** How many counters? Write the number.

School-Home Letter

Dear Family,

My class started Chapter 6 today. I will learn all about the number 20. I will learn how to model, read and write 20, and how to count forward and backward from 20.

Love, _____

Vocabulary

twenty a number one more than nineteen

20

Home Activity

Grab a pack of number flash cards and ask your child to lay out 20 cards to model what 20 looks like. Then ask your child to place the number cards in the correct order from 1 to 20. For a challenge, see if your child can order the cards from 20 to 1.

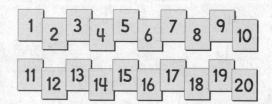

Literature

Look for these books at the library. Your child will enjoy great illustrations while learning more about the number 20.

20 Hungry Piggies by Trudy Harris. Millbrook Press, 2006.

Counting 1–20 by Lesley Clark. Ladybird Books, 1999.

Carta
para la **casa**

Querida familia:

Mi clase comenzó hoy el Capítulo 6. Aprenderé todo sobre el número 20. Aprenderé a representar, leer y escribir 20 y a contar hacia adelante y hacia atrás desde 20.

Con cariño, _____

Vocabulario

veinte uno más que diecinueve

20

Actividad para la casa

Tome un paquete de tarjetas de vocabulario y pida a su hijo que separe 20 tarjetas para representar un conjunto de 20. Luego pídale que ponga las tarjetas del 1 al 20 en el orden correcto. Después, anímelo a ordenar las tarjetas del 20 al 1.

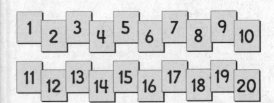

Literatura

Busquen estos libros en la biblioteca. Su hijo disfrutará de las coloridas ilustraciones mientras aprende más sobre el número 20.

20 Hungry Piggies
por Trudy Harris.
Millbrook Press, 2006.

Counting 1–20
por Lesley Clark
Ladybird Books, 1999.

Name _____

Model 20

DIRECTIONS **1.** Use counters to show the number 20. Draw the counters. **2.** Circle to show 20 beads on the bead string.

Chapter 6

one hundred twenty-nine **P129**

Lesson Check

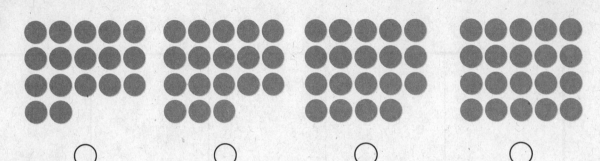

○ ○ ○ ○

Spiral Review

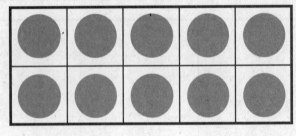
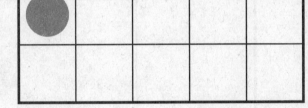

9   10   11   12

○   ○   ○   ○

5   6   7   8

○   ○   ○   ○

DIRECTIONS 1. Which set shows 20 objects? Mark under your answer. **(Lesson 6.1)   2.** Count and tell how many counters are in the ten frames. Mark under your answer. **(Lesson 5.1)   3.** How many basketballs in all? Mark under your answer. **(Lesson 4.3)**

Name _____

Read and Write 20

 1

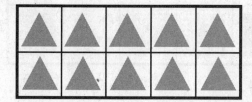 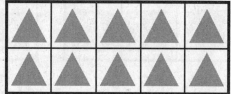
_____
- - - - - - - - - - - -
_____

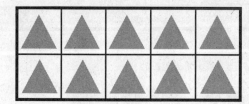 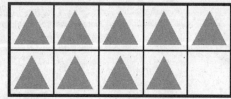
_____
- - - - - - - - - - - -
_____

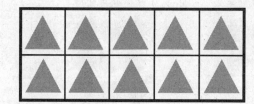 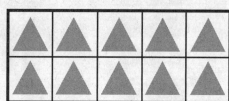
_____
- - - - - - - - - - - -
_____

- -

2

19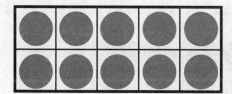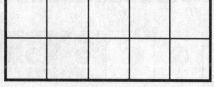
_____
- - - - - - - - - - - -
_____

20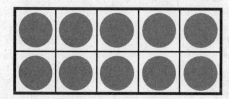
_____
- - - - - - - - - - - -
_____

DIRECTIONS   1. Count and tell how many triangles. Write the numbers.   **2.** Draw more counters to show the numbers. Write the numbers.

Chapter 6

Lesson Check

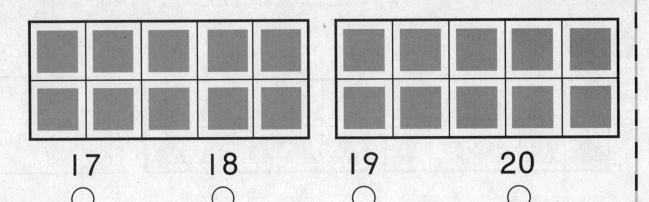

17   18   19   20
○   ○   ○   ○

Spiral Review

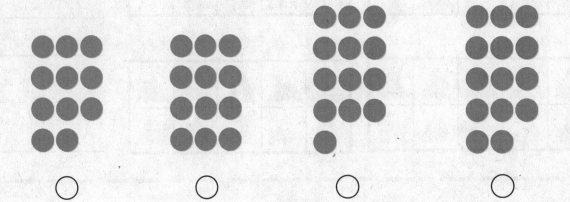

○   ○   ○   ○

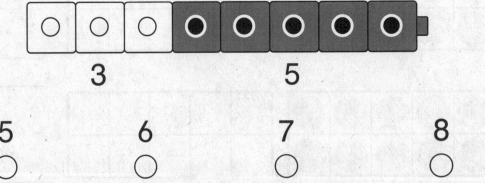

3   5

5   6   7   8
○   ○   ○   ○

DIRECTIONS **1.** Count and tell how many squares are in the ten frames. Mark under your answer. **(Lesson 6.2)** **2.** Which set has 13 objects? Mark under your answer. **(Lesson 5.3)** **3.** How many cubes in all? Mark under your answer. **(Lesson 4.2)**

Name _____

Make a Model • Compare Numbers to 20

DIRECTIONS **1.** Teni has 16 berries. She has two more berries than Marta. Use cubes to model the sets of berries. Compare the sets. Which set has more cubes? Draw the cubes. Write how many in each set. Circle the greater number. **2.** Ben has 18 marbles. Sophia has two fewer marbles than Ben. Use cubes to model the sets of marbles. Compare the sets. Which set has more cubes? Draw the cubes. Write how many in each set. Circle the number that is less.

© Houghton Mifflin Harcourt Publishing Company

Chapter 6

one hundred thirty-three **P133**

Lesson Check

○   ○   ○   ○

Spiral Review

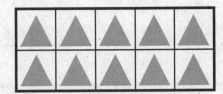   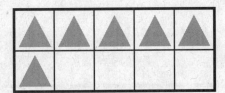

14   15   16   17

○   ○   ○   ○

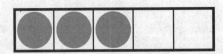

   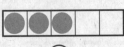      

○   ○   ○   ○

DIRECTIONS 1. Compare the sets. Which set has 3 fewer than 20? Mark under your answer. **(Lesson 6.3)** 2. Count and tell how many. Mark under your answer. **(Lesson 5.7)** 3. Count and tell how many counters are in the five frame. Mark under the set of counters that shows one more counter. **(Lesson 2.2)**

Name _____

Count and Order Numbers to 20

 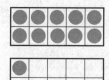 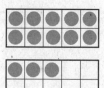

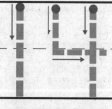 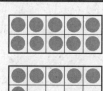 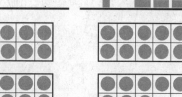 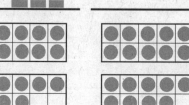

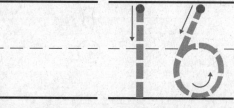

DIRECTIONS **1.** Count the dots in the ten frames. Trace or write the numbers. **2.** Write those numbers in order.

Lesson Check

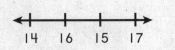 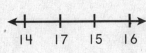 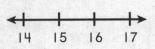 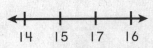

14 16 15 17   14 17 15 16   14 15 16 17   14 15 17 16

○   ○   ○   ○

Spiral Review

$$3 + 4 = \underline{\quad}$$

4   6   7   8
○   ○   ○   ○

four   five   six   seven
○   ○   ○   ○

DIRECTIONS **1.** Which number line shows the numbers in the correct order? Mark under your answer. (Lesson 6.4) **2.** How many books in all? Mark under your answer. (Lesson 4.5) **3.** How many erasers? Mark under your answer. (Lesson 1.4)

P136 one hundred thirty-six

Count Forward and Backward

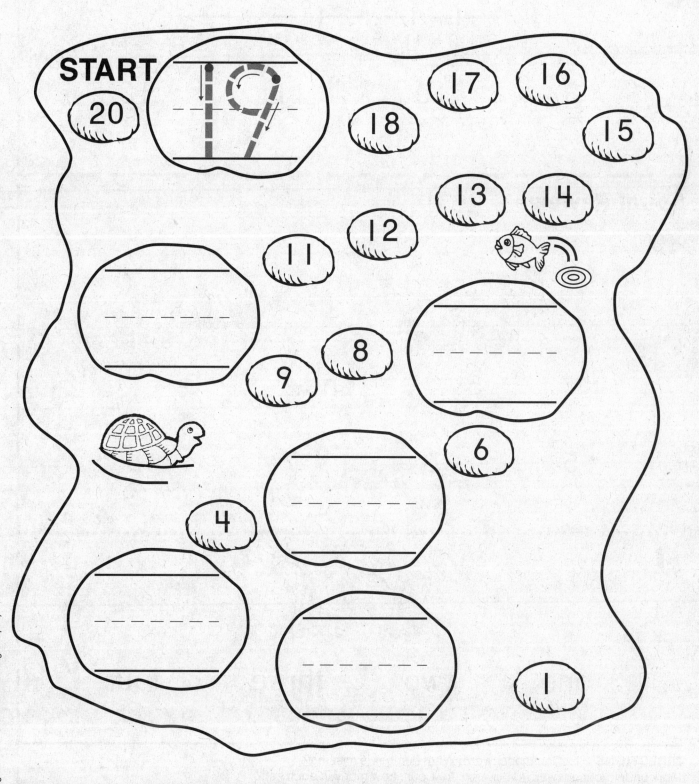

START
20

19

18   17   16   15

13   14

12

11

____
- - -
____

9   8   ____

6

4   ____
- - -
____

____
- - -
____

____
- - -
____

1

DIRECTIONS I. Count backward. Write the missing numbers.

Lesson Check

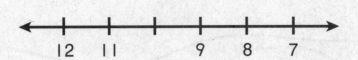

| 12 | 11 | | 9 | 8 | 7 |

8
○

10
○

11
○

13
○

Spiral Review

5   and   3

5
○

6
○

7
○

8
○

one
○

two
○

three
○

four
○

DIRECTIONS   1. Count backward. What number is missing?
Mark under your answer. (Lesson 6.5)   **2.** Count how many in each set.
How many raccoons in all? Mark under your answer. (Lesson 4.3)   **3.** How
many skunks? Mark under your answer. (Lesson 1.2)

Name _____

Numbers 21 to 31

1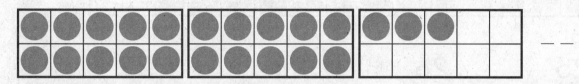

_____

- - - - - - - - - - - - - - - - - - - -

2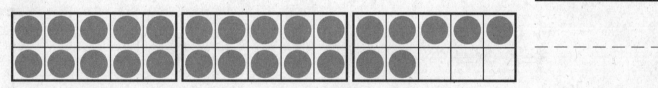

_____

- - - - - - - - - - - - - - - - - - - -

3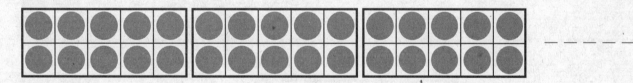

_____

- - - - - - - - - - - - - - - - - - - -

4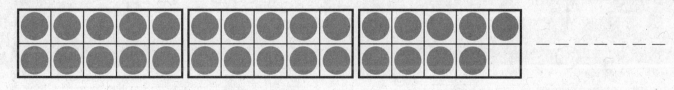

_____

DIRECTIONS 1–4. How many counters? Write the number.

Lesson Check

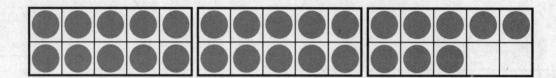

25	26	28	29
○	○	○	○

Spiral Review

2	3	4	5
○	○	○	○

1	2	3	4
○	○	○	○

DIRECTIONS **1.** How many counters? Mark under your answer.
(Lesson 6.6) **2.** How many crabs are left? Mark under you answer. (Lesson 4.10)
3. 8 is how many more than 5? Mark under your answer. (Lesson 3.5)

Name _____

Count to 100

1	2	3	4	5	6	7	8	9	10
11	12	13	14	15	16	17	18	19	20
21	22	23	24	25	26	27	28	29	30
31	32	33	34	35	36	37	38	39	40
41	42	43	44	45	46	47	48	49	50
51	52	53	54	55	56	57	58	59	60
61	62	63	64	65	66	67	68	69	70
71	72	73	74	75	76	77	78	79	80
81	82	83	84	85	86	87	88	89	90
91	92	93	94	95	96	97	98	99	100

DIRECTIONS **1.** Point to each number as you count to 100. Mark an X on 20. Begin with 20 and count forward to 30. Circle the number 30.

Lesson Check

1	2	3	4	5	6	7	8	9	10
11	12	13	14	15	16	17	18	19	20
21	22	23	24	25	26	27	28	29	30

20   21   22   23
○   ○   ○   ○

Spiral Review

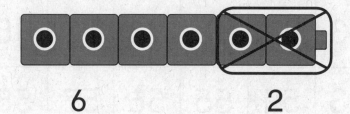

6   2

2   3   4   5
○   ○   ○   ○

○   ○   ○   ○

DIRECTIONS **1.** Begin with 1 and count forward to 20. What is the next number? Mark under your answer. **(Lesson 6.7)** **2.** How many are left? Mark under your answer. **(Lesson 4.9)** **3.** Count and tell how many trees. Which set of flowers has the same number? Mark under your answer. **(Lesson 2.1)**

Use a Hundred Chart

1	2	3	4	5	6	7	8	9	10
11	12	13	14	15	16	17	18	19	20
21	22	23	24	25	26	27	28	29	30
31	32	33	34	35	36	37	38	39	40
41	42	43	44	45	46	47	48	49	50
51	52	53	54	55	56	57	58	59	60
61	62	63	64	65	66	67	68	69	70
71	72	73	74	75	76	77	78	79	80
81	82	83	84	85	86	87	88	89	90
91	92	93	94	95	96	97	98	99	100

DIRECTIONS   1. Circle each number on the hundred chart that ends in a 5. Tell what you know about these numbers. Mark an X on each number on the hundred chart that ends in a 0. Tell what you know about these numbers.

Lesson Check

1

1	2	3	4	5	6	7	8	9	10
11	12	13	14	15	16	17	18	19	20
21	22	23	24	25	26	27	28	29	30

0 ○   1 ○   5 ○   9 ○

Spiral Review

2

16 ○   17 ○   18 ○   19 ○

3

2 ○   3 ○   4 ○   5 ○

DIRECTIONS **1.** Look at the shaded boxes. Which number do all of the numbers in the shaded boxes end with? Mark under your answer. **(Lesson 6.8)**
2. How many cubes? Mark under your answer. **(Lesson 5.7)** **3.** Which number shows how many crayons? Mark under your answer. **(Lesson 1.6)**

Counting Tens

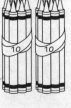

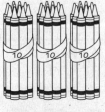

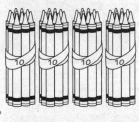

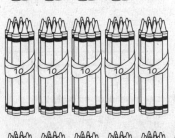

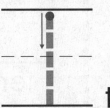 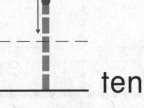 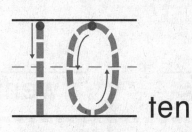

_____ ten   _____ ten

_____ tens   _____ twenty

_____ tens   _____ thirty

_____ tens   _____ forty

_____ tens   _____ fifty

_____ tens   _____ sixty

_____ tens   _____ seventy

DIRECTIONS   **I.** Write how many tens. Write the number. Read the number and the word.

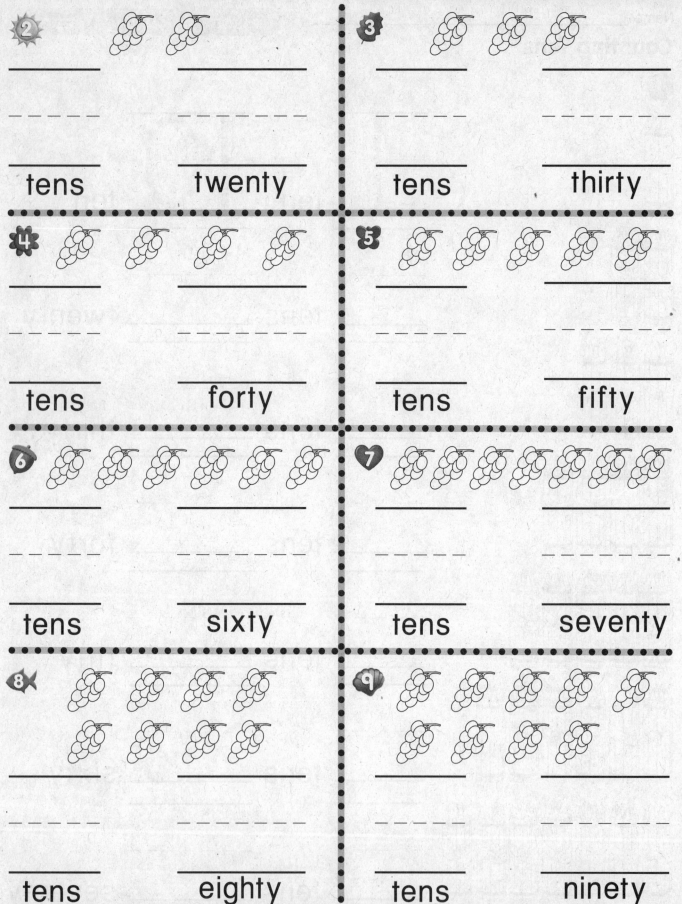

2 _____ _____ _____

_____ _____

tens   **twenty**

3 _____ _____

_____ _____

tens   **thirty**

4 _____ _____

_____ _____

tens   **forty**

5 _____ _____

_____ _____

tens   **fifty**

6 _____ _____

_____ _____

tens   **sixty**

7 _____ _____

_____ _____

tens   **seventy**

8 _____ _____

_____ _____

tens   **eighty**

9 _____ _____

_____ _____

tens   **ninety**

DIRECTIONS   **2–9.** Write how many tens. Write the number. Read the number and the word.

P144b   one hundred forty-four

Tens and Ones

 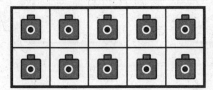 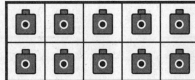 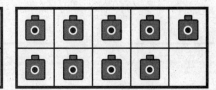

2 tens 　　 9 ones 　　 _____

 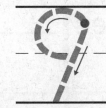

_____ tens 　　 _____ ones 　　 _____

_____ tens 　　 _____ ones 　　 _____

DIRECTIONS 1. How many tens? Trace the number. How many ones? Trace the number. Write the number. **2–3.** How many tens? How many ones? Write the number.

4

_____   _____

- - - - - - -   - - - - - - -

_____ tens _____ ones

          _____

          - - - - - - -

          _____

5

_____   _____

- - - - - - -   - - - - - - -

_____ tens _____ ones

          _____

          - - - - - - -

          _____

6

_____   _____

- - - - - - -   - - - - - - -

_____ tens _____ ones

          _____

          - - - - - - -

          _____

7

_____   _____

- - - - - - -   - - - - - - -

_____ tens _____ ones

          _____

          - - - - - - -

          _____

DIRECTIONS 4–7. How many tens? How many ones? Write the number.

P144d one hundred forty-four

Chapter 6 Extra Practice

Lessons 6.1 – 6.3 (pp. 265 – 276)

 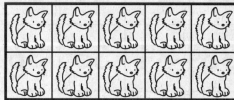

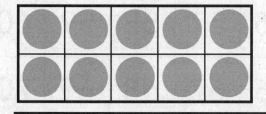

DIRECTIONS **1.** Circle to show 20 beads on the bead string. **2.** Count and tell how how many dogs. Write the number. **3.** Use more counters to model the number that is 3 fewer than 20. Write that number. Draw and color the counters.

1	2	3	4	5	6	7	8	9	10
11	12	13	14	15	16	17	18	19	20
21	22	23	24	25	26	27	28	29	30
31	32	33	34	35	36	37	38	39	40
41	42	43	44	45	46	47	48	49	50
51	52	53	54	55	56	57	58	59	60
61	62	63	64	65	66	67	68	69	70
71	72	73	74	75	76	77	78	79	80
81	82	83	84	85	86	87	88	89	90
91	92	93	94	95	96	97	98	99	100

DIRECTIONS   1. Point to each number as you count to 100. Circle the number 10. Begin with 10 and count forward to 31. Circle the number 31. Mark an X on each number on the hundred chart that ends in 5. Tell what you know about these numbers.

School-Home Letter

Dear Family,

My class started Chapter 7 today. In the next few lessons, I will learn all about sorting and graphing. I will learn how to sort by color, shape, and size. I will also learn how to make and read a graph.

Love, _____

Vocabulary

sort

These bears are sorted by size. One set is small, and one set is large.

Home Activity

Have some fun in the kitchen as your child shows you all about sorting. Begin by grabbing a handful of silverware. Have your child sort it into groups by type of utensil.

Literature

Look for this book at the library. Your child will continue learning while enjoying this great book.

Sorting
by Henry Arthur Pluckrose. Children's Press, 1995.

Carta para la casa

Querida familia:

Mi clase comenzó hoy el Capítulo 7. En las próximas lecciones, aprenderé todo sobre la clasificación y las gráficas. Aprenderé a clasificar según el color, la forma y el tamaño. También aprenderé a hacer y leer una gráfica.

Con cariño, _____

Vocabulario

clasificar

Estos osos se clasifican según el tamaño. Un grupo es pequeño y el otro es grande.

Actividad para la casa

Organicen una actividad divertida en la cocina, para que su hijo practique la clasificación. Tome unos cubiertos y pida a su hijo que los clasifique según el tipo de utensilio.

Literatura

Busquen este libro en la biblioteca. Su hijo seguirá aprendiendo mientras disfruta de este libro divertido.

Sorting
por Henry Arthur Pluckrose. Children's Press, 1995.

Name _____

Algebra: Sort and Describe by Color

DIRECTIONS 1–4. Look at the set of shapes at the beginning of the row. Tell how the shapes are sorted. Circle the shape that belongs in the set.

Lesson Check

○   ○   ○   ○

Spiral Review

eleven   twelve   thirteen   fourteen

4   5   6   7

○   ○   ○   ○

DIRECTIONS I. Look at the set of shapes. Which shape belongs in the set? Mark under your answer. (Lesson 7.1) **2.** How many coats? Mark under your answer. (Lesson 5.4) **3.** How many umbrellas? Mark under your answer. (Lesson 3.3)

Algebra: Sort and Describe by Shape

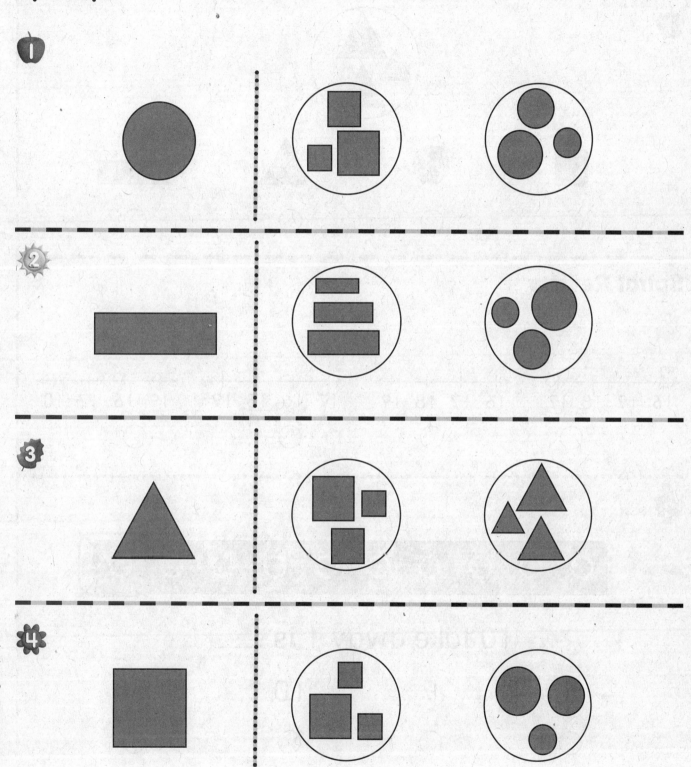

DIRECTIONS 1–4. Look at the shape at the beginning of the row. Tell what you know about the shape. Mark an X on the set in which the shape belongs.

Chapter 7

one hundred fifty-one **P151**

○   ○   ○   ○

Spiral Review

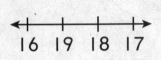 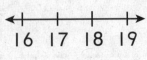 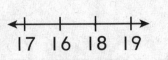 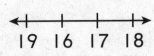

| 16 19 18 17 | 16 17 18 19 | 17 16 18 19 | 19 16 17 18 |

 ○   ○   ○   ○

10 take away 1 is ___

5	9	10	11
○	○	○	○

DIRECTIONS   1. Which shape belongs in the set? Mark under your answer. **(Lesson 7.2)   2.** Which number line shows the numbers in the correct order? Mark under your answer. **(Lesson 6.4)   3.** How many are left? Mark under your answer. **(Lesson 4.10)**

Algebra: Sort and Describe by Size

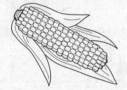  

DIRECTIONS I–4. Mark an X on the object that does not belong.

Lesson Check

1

○   ○   ○   ○

Spiral Review

2

12	13	14	15
○	○	○	○

3

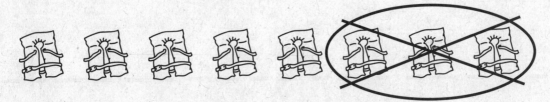

$$8 - 3 = \underline{\quad}$$

2	3	4	5
○	○	○	○

DIRECTIONS 1. Which shape does not belong? Mark under your answer. (Lesson 7.3) 2. Count and tell how many ants. Mark under your answer. (Lesson 5.3) 3. Which number completes the subtraction sentence? Mark under your answer. (Lesson 4.13)

Name _____

Make a Graph • Concrete Graphs

①

②

How Many of Each Shape?				

③

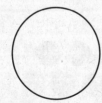  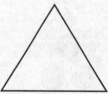

DIRECTIONS 1. Place a handful of small green shapes on the workspace. 2. Sort the shapes. Move the shapes to the graph. Draw and color the shapes. 3. Write how many of each shape. Which has the fewest shapes? Circle that shape.

Lesson Check

How Many of Each Counter?

○   ○   ○   ○

Spiral Review

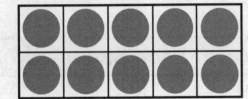 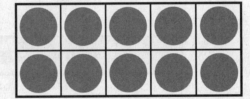

17   18   19   20

○   ○   ○   ○

 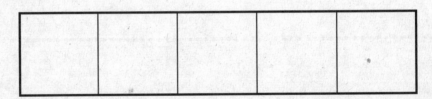

DIRECTIONS **1.** Which row has more counters? Mark under your answer. (Lesson 7.4)
2. How many counters? Mark under your answer. (Lesson 6.1) **3.** Trace the number.
How many counters would you place in the five frame? Mark under your answer (Lesson 1.5)

P156 one hundred fifty-six

Read a Picture Graph

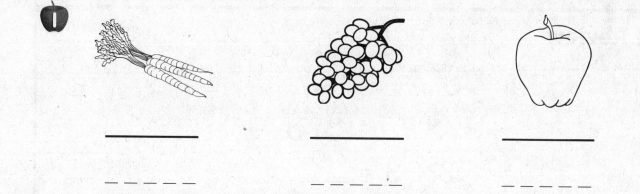

Favorite Snacks					
🍎	☺	☺	☺	☺	☺
🍇	☺				
🥕	☺	☺	☺	☺	

      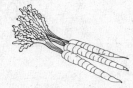

_____   _____   _____

- - - - - - - - -   - - - - - - - - -   - - - - - - - - -

_____   _____   _____

2

DIRECTIONS **1.** Read the graph. Write how many children like each kind of snack. **2.** Circle the snack that the most children like.

Lesson Check

1

Shapes			
☺	☺	☺	
☺	☺	☺	☺
☺	☺		

◯   ◯   ◯   ◯

Spiral Review

2

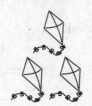 

$$3 + 3 = \underline{}$$

4   5   6   7

◯   ◯   ◯   ◯

3

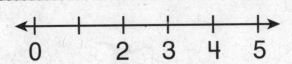

0   1   2   3

◯   ◯   ◯   ◯

DIRECTIONS **1.** Which shape do the most children like? Mark under your answer. (Lesson 7.5) **2.** How many kites in all? Mark under your answer. (Lesson 4.5) **3.** What number comes after 0? Mark under your answer. (Lesson 2.6)

Make a Picture Graph

1

Which Kind of Animal Are More People Watching?				
☺	☺	☺	☺	☺
☺	☺	☺		

2

_____

- - - - - - - - -

_____

- - - - - - - - -

DIRECTIONS **1.** Look at the picture. Make a picture graph to show how many people are watching each animal. Which row has the fewest children? Circle that row. **2.** Write how many people are watching each animal. Circle the greatest number.

Lesson Check

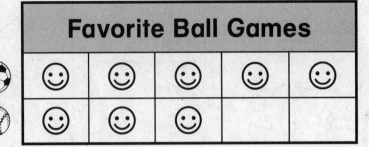

Favorite Ball Games

○ ○ ○ ○

Spiral Review

II

eleven

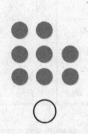 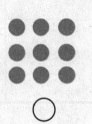  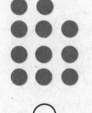

○ ○ ○ ○

10 take away 3 is ___

4   5   6   7

○   ○   ○   ○

DIRECTIONS 1. Which ball game do more children like best? Mark under your answer. (Lesson 7.6) 2. Which set shows 11 objects? Mark under your answer. (Lesson 5.1) 3. How many ducks are left? Mark under your answer. (Lesson 4.10)

Chapter 7 Extra Practice

Lessons 7.1 – 7.3 (pp. 313–324) . . . .

Big   **Triangle**

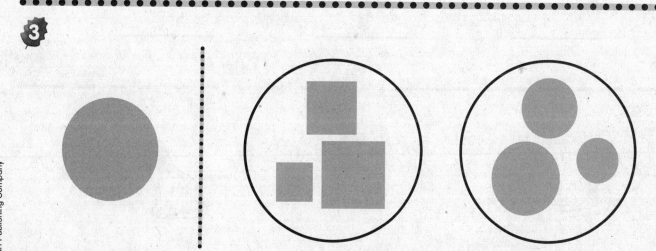

DIRECTIONS 1. Sort a handful of shapes by size and shape. Draw the shapes. **2.** What shape is in both spaces in the workmats above? Draw and color that shape. **3.** Look at the shape at the beginning of the row. Tell what you know about the shape. Mark an X on the set where the shape belongs.

Favorite Pet				
 ☺	☺	☺		
☺	☺	☺	☺	
☺	☺			

   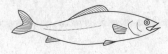

_____   _____   _____

- - - - - - - - - - -   - - - - - - - - - - -   - - - - - - - - - - -

_____   _____   _____

   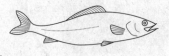

DIRECTIONS **1.** Read the graph. Write how many children like each kind of pet. **2.** Circle the pet that the fewest children like.

School-Home Letter

Dear Family,

My class started Chapter 8 today. In the next few lessons, I will learn about two-dimensional shapes. I will also learn how to combine shapes to make new shapes.

Love, _____

Vocabulary

curve a line that is not straight

vertex corner

 ← vertex

Home Activity

Spread out a group of household objects and have your child point out the objects that look like squares and circles and triangles.

Literature

Look for these books at the library. The pictures and stories will capture your child's imagination.

Captain Invincible and the Space Shapes by Stuart J. Murphy. HarperCollins Publishers, 2001.

Shapes, Shapes, Shapes by Tana Hoban. HarperTrophy, 1996.

Carta
para la casa

Querida familia:

Mi clase comenzó hoy el Capítulo 8. En las próximas lecciones, aprenderé sobre las figuras bidimensionales. También aprenderé a combinar las figuras para formar figuras diferentes.

Con cariño, _____

Vocabulario

curva una línea que no es recta

vértice esquina

←———— vértice

Actividad para la casa

Dé a su hijo varios objetos que encuentre en la casa y pídale que señale los que se parezcan a los cuadrados, círculos y triángulos.

¡Viva nuestro equipo!

Literatura

Busquen estos libros en la biblioteca. Las ilustraciones y los relatos estimularán la imaginación de su hijo.

Captain Invincible and the Space Shapes por Stuart J. Murphy. HarperCollins Publishers, 2001.

Shapes, Shapes, Shapes por Tana Hoban. HarperTrophy, 1996.

Identify and Name Squares

1

DIRECTIONS 1. Color the squares in the picture.

○   ○   ○   ○

Spiral Review

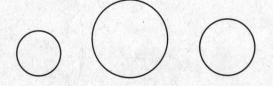

○   ○   ○   ○

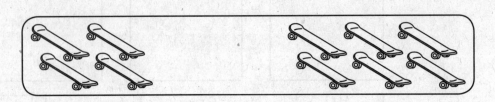

4 and 6 is ____

12   11   10   9

○   ○   ○   ○

DIRECTIONS   1. Which shape is a square? Mark under your answer.
(Lesson 8.1)   2. Which shape belongs in the set? Mark under your answer. **(Lesson 7.2)   3.** How many in all? Mark under your answer.
(Lesson 4.3)

Describe Squares

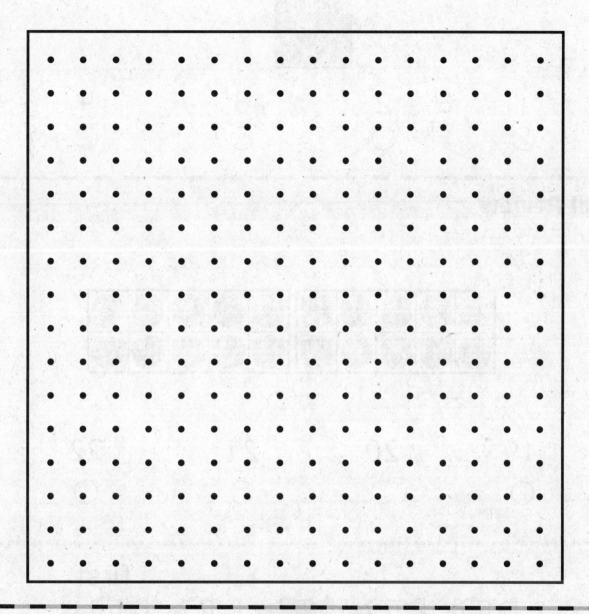

© Houghton Mifflin Harcourt Publishing Company

2 _____ _____ **vertices**

3 _____ _____ **sides**

DIRECTIONS 1. Draw and color a square. 2. Mark an X on each corner, or vertex of the square that you drew. Write how many corners or vertices. 3. Trace around the sides of the square that you drew. Write how many sides.

Lesson Check

1

1	2	3	4
○	○	○	○

Spiral Review

2

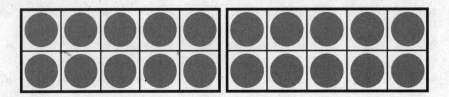

19	20	21	22
○	○	○	○

3

first

first	second	third	fourth
○	○	○	○

DIRECTIONS 1. How many vertices does the square have? Mark under your answer. (Lesson 8.2) 2. Count and tell how many. Mark under your answer. (Lesson 6.2) 3. Which fish is shaded? Mark under your answer. (Lesson 2.7)

Identify and Name Triangles

DIRECTIONS 1–2. Color the triangles in the picture.

Chapter 8

Lesson Check

 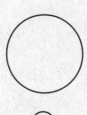

Spiral Review

  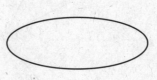

DIRECTIONS **1.** Which shape is a triangle? Mark under your answer. **(Lesson 8.3)** **2.** Which shape belongs in the set? Mark under your answer. **(Lesson 6.1)** **3.** Count and tell how many leaves. Which set of counters has one fewer? Mark under your answer. **(Lesson 2.3)**

P170 one hundred seventy

Name _____

Describe Triangles

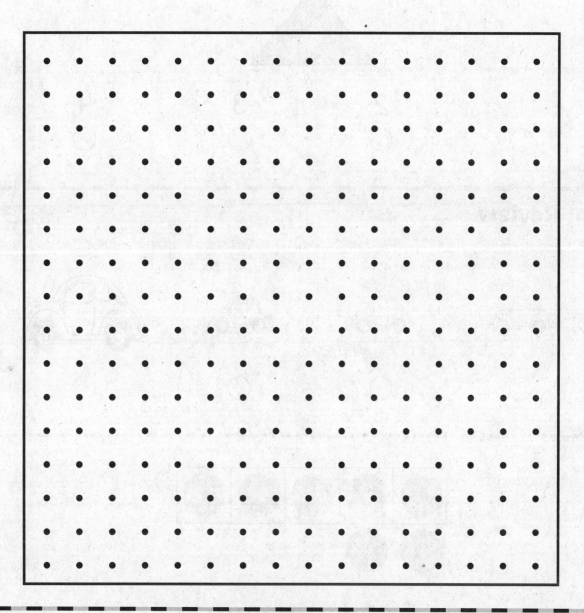

_____ vertices ⋮ _____ sides

DIRECTIONS 1. Draw and color a triangle. 2. Mark an X on each corner, or vertex of the triangle that you drew. Write how many corners, or vertices. 3. Trace around the sides of the triangle that you drew. Write how many sides.

Chapter 8

❶

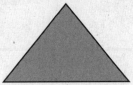

| 1 | 2 | 3 | 4 |
| ○ | ○ | ○ | ○ |

Spiral Review

○ ○ ○ ○

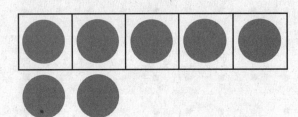

5 and ___ more

| 1 | 2 | 3 | 4 |
| ○ | ○ | ○ | ○ |

DIRECTIONS **1.** How many sides does the triangle have? Mark under your answer. **(Lesson 8.4)** **2.** Which object does not belong? Mark under your answer. **(Lesson 7.3)** **3.** How many more than 5 is 7? Mark under your answer. **(Lesson 3.3)**

Identify and Name Circles

 1

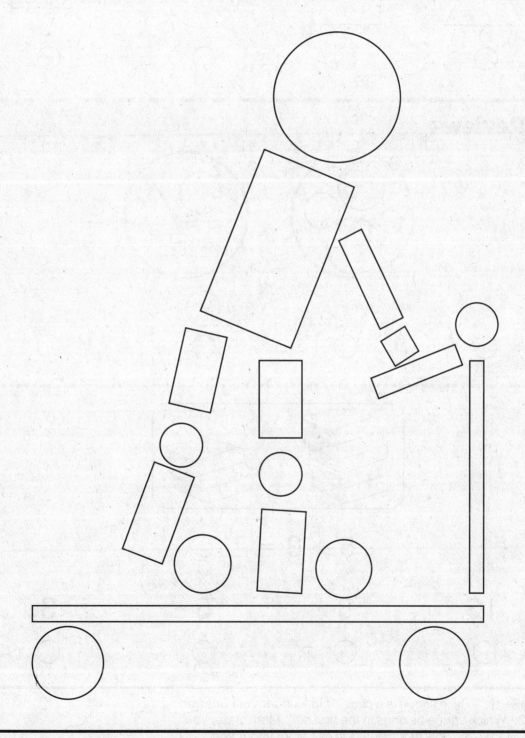

DIRECTIONS 1. Color the circles in the picture.

Lesson Check

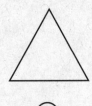  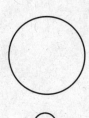

○   ○   ○   ○

Spiral Review

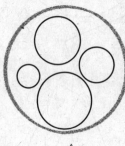   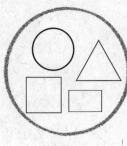

○   ○   ○   ○

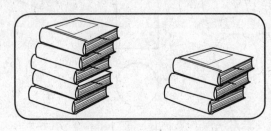

$$5 + 3 = \underline{}$$

13   8   5   3

○   ○   ○   ○

DIRECTIONS   **1.** Which shape is a circle? Mark under your answer. (Lesson 8.5)   **2.** Which shape belongs in the first set? Mark under your answer. (Lesson 7.2)   **3.** How many books in all? Mark under your answer. (Lesson 4.5)

Describe Circles

1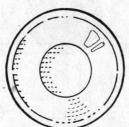

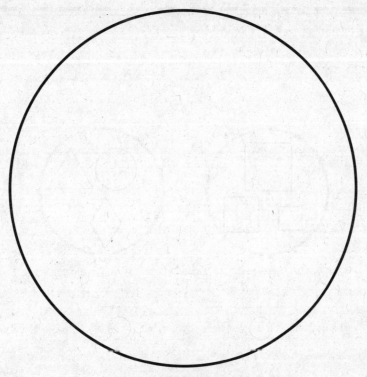

circle

2 _____   **3** _____

- - - - -   - - - - -

_____ vertices   _____ straight sides

DIRECTIONS **1.** Color the object that is shaped like a circle. **2.** Look at the circle. Place a counter on each corner, or vertex. Write how many corners, or vertices. **3.** Place a counter on each straight side. Write how many straight sides.

Lesson Check

0   1   3   4
○   ○   ○   ○

Spiral Review

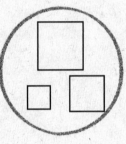   

○   ○   ○   ○

○   ○   ○   ○

DIRECTIONS **1.** How many vertices does the circle have? Mark under your answer. (Lesson 8.6) **2.** Which shape belongs in the first set? Mark under your answer. (Lesson 7.2) **3.** Which set of cubes shows 16? Mark under your answer. (Lesson 5.7)

Identify and Name Rectangles

1

DIRECTIONS **1.** Color the rectangles in the picture.

Lesson Check

Spiral Review

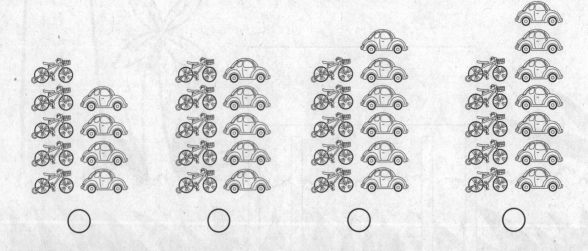

DIRECTIONS **1.** Which shape is a rectangle? Mark under your answer.
(Lesson 8.7) **2.** Which animal do more children like? Mark under your
answer. (Lesson 7.5) **3.** Which picture shows fewer cars than bikes? Mark
under your answer. (Lesson 2.3)

Describe Rectangles

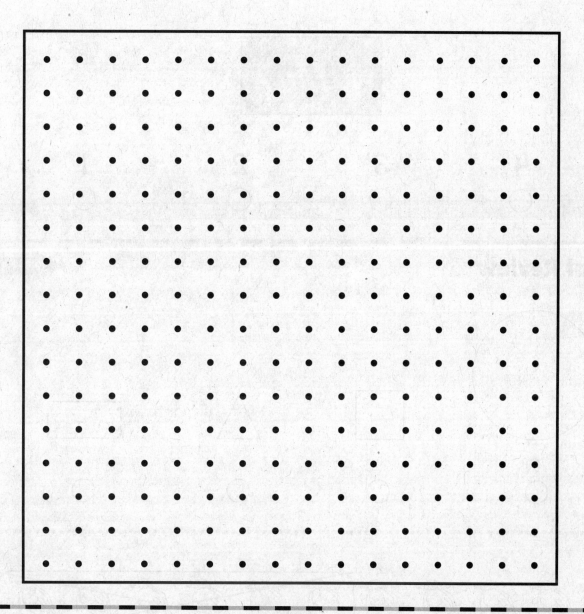

2 _____

_ _ _ _ _

_____ vertices

3 _____

_ _ _ _ _

_____ sides

DIRECTIONS 1. Draw and color a rectangle. 2. Mark an X on each corner, or vertex of the rectangle that you drew. Write how many corners, or vertices. 3. Trace around the sides of the rectangle that you drew. Write how many sides.

Lesson Check

1

4	3	2	1
○	○	○	○

Spiral Review

2

○	○	○	○

3

2	3	4	5
○	○	○	○

DIRECTIONS **1.** How many sides does the rectangle have? Mark under your answer. **(Lesson 8.8)** **2.** Which shape does not belong? Mark under your answer. **(Lesson 7.3)** **3.** How many birds are left? Mark under your answer. **(Lesson 4.10)**

Algebra: Sort Two-Dimensional Shapes

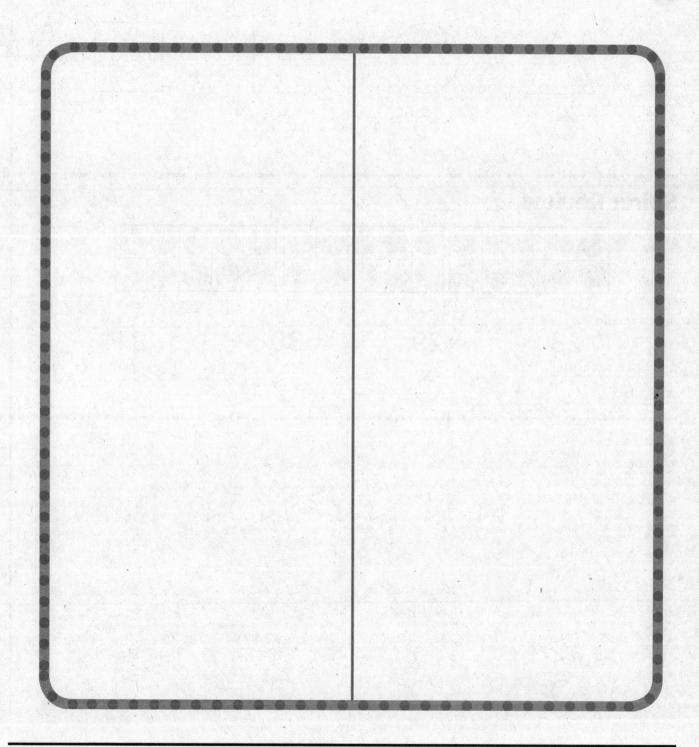

DIRECTIONS **1.** Place a handful of shapes on the page. Listen to the sorting rule. Sort the shapes by the number of sides. Draw the shapes on the sorting mat.

Chapter 8

Lesson Check

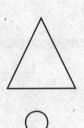         

   ◯   ◯   ◯   ◯

Spiral Review

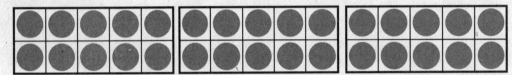

28   **29**   **30**   **31**

  ◯   ◯   ◯   ◯

  ◯   ◯   ◯   ◯

DIRECTIONS   **1.** Which shape has three vertices? Mark under your answer. **(Lesson 8.9)**   **2.** How many counters? Mark under your answer. **(Lesson 6.6)**   **3.** Count and tell how many stars. Which set of stars has 1 more? Mark under your answer. **(Lesson 2.2)**

Name _____

Identify and Describe Other Shapes

trapezoid

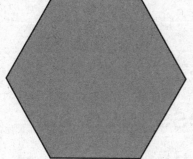

hexagon

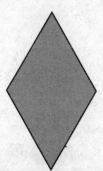

rhombus

DIRECTIONS 1–3. Place a shape that matches beside the shape. Draw and color the shape. Describe the shape. Tell the name of the shape.

Chapter 8

one hundred eighty-three **P183**

Lesson Check

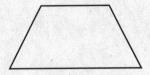

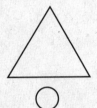  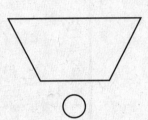 

○   ○   ○   ○

Spiral Review

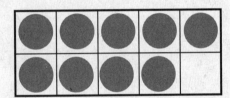   9 is _____ less than 10

1   2   3   4

○   ○   ○   ○

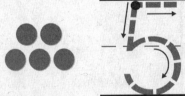

○   ○   ○   ○

DIRECTIONS   **1.** Which shape is the same as the trapezoid shown? Mark under your answer. **(Lesson 8.10)**   **2.** 9 is how many less than 10? Mark under your answer. **(Lesson 3.7)**
3. Count the counters. Which set shows fewer? Mark under your answer. **(Lesson 2.4)**

P184   one hundred eighty-four

Draw a Picture • Combine Shapes

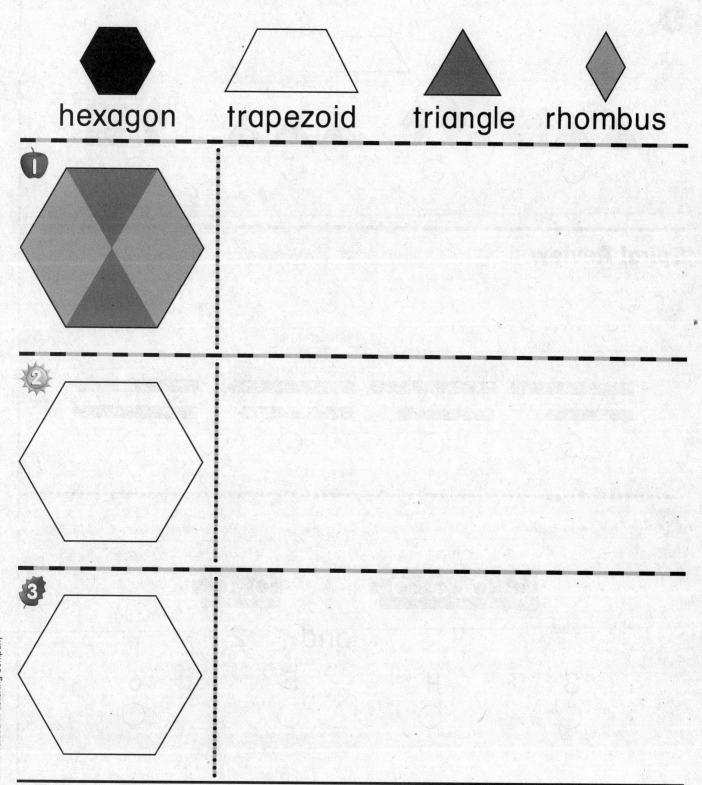

hexagon   trapezoid   triangle   rhombus

DIRECTIONS 1. How can you use the rhombus shapes and the triangle shapes to cover the outline of the hexagon? Draw and color the shapes. **2–3.** Draw other ways to use the shapes to cover the outline of the hexagon.

Lesson Check

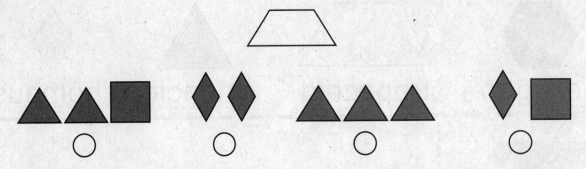

○   ○   ○   ○

Spiral Review

○   ○   ○   ○

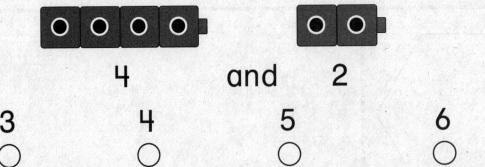

4   and   2

3   4   5   6

○   ○   ○   ○

DIRECTIONS I. Which shapes could you use to cover the trapezoid? Mark under your answer. **(Lesson 8.11)** 2. Which set has 20 cubes? Mark under your answer. **(Lesson 6.1)** 3. How many cubes in all? Mark under your answer. **(Lesson 4.3)**

Name _____

Symmetry

1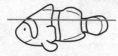

2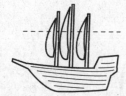

3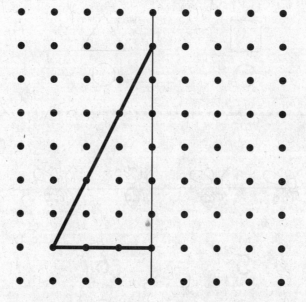

DIRECTIONS 1–2. Circle the objects with a line of symmetry that makes two matching parts. 3. Complete the triangle that would show the line of symmetry.

Lesson Check

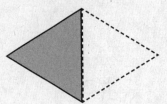

Spiral Review

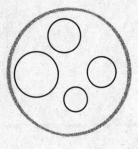 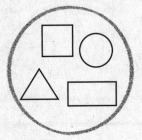

4   5   6   7

○   ○   ○   ○

DIRECTIONS I. Which shape completes the picture to show a line of symmetry with two matching parts? Mark under your answer. (Lesson 8.12)   2. Which shape is in both sorting rings? Mark under your answer. (Lesson 7.2)   3. How many bees? Mark under your answer. (Lesson 3.2)

P188 one hundred eighty-eight

Chapter 8 Extra Practice

Lessons 8.1 – 8.4 (pp. 345–360) ·

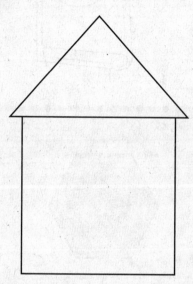

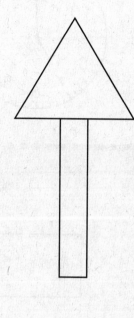

· ·

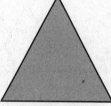
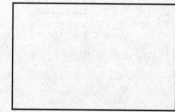

· ·

DIRECTIONS **1.** Use red to color the squares in the picture.
Use green to color the triangles. **2.** Which shape is a square?
Mark an X on that shape. Which shapes are triangles? Circle those
shapes. **3.** I have 3 sides and 3 vertices. What shape am I? Draw
the shape. Tell about your shape.

© Houghton Mifflin Harcourt Publishing Company

Lessons 8.5 – 8.12 (pp. 361–392)

1

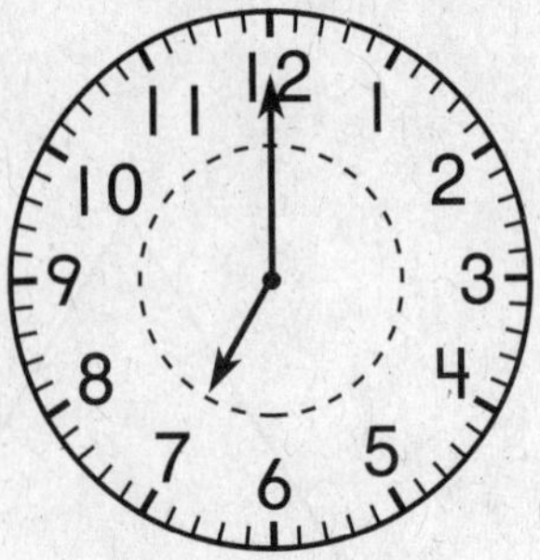

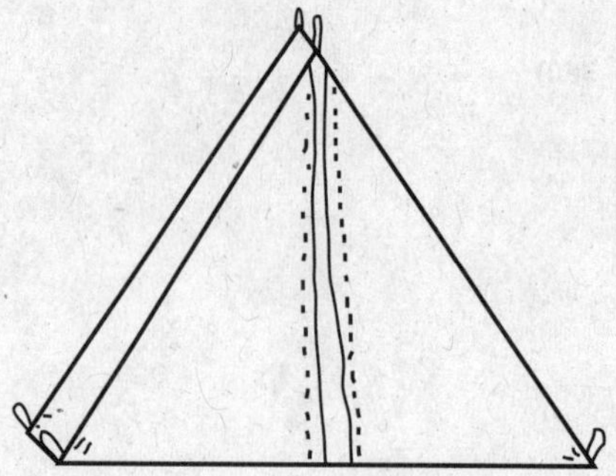

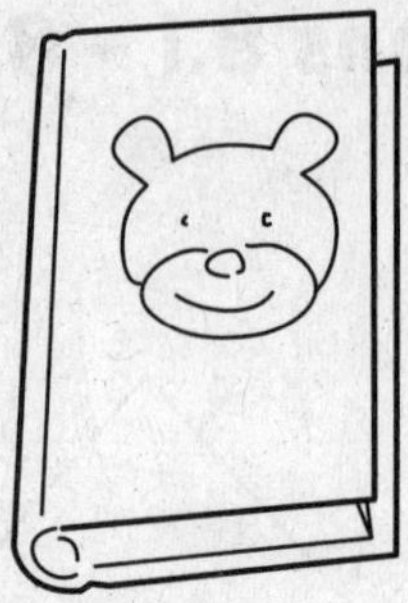

2

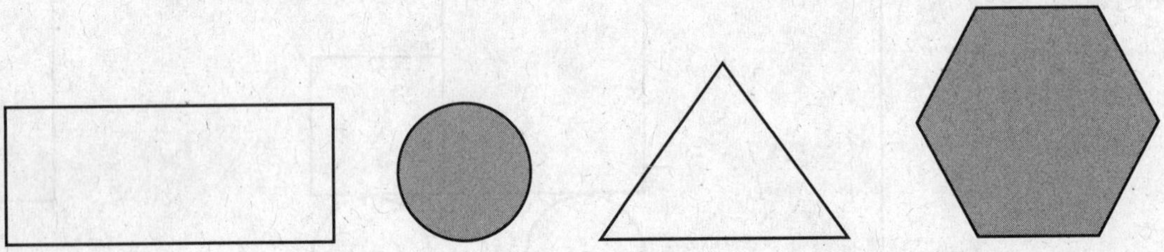

3

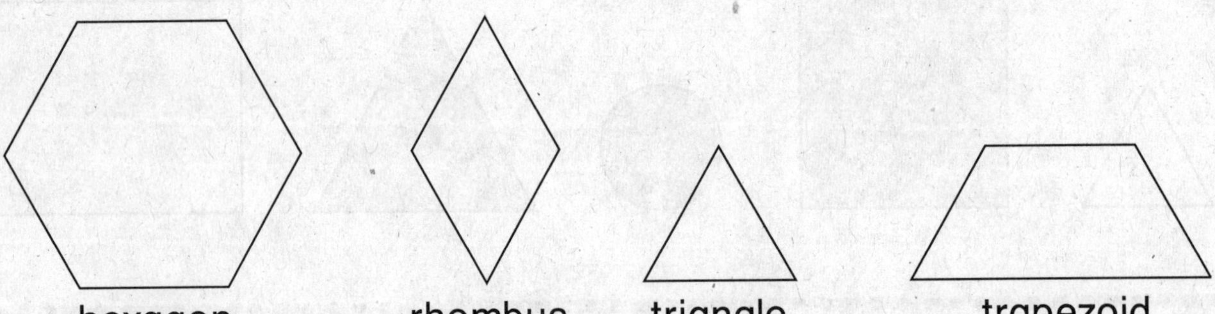

hexagon rhombus triangle trapezoid

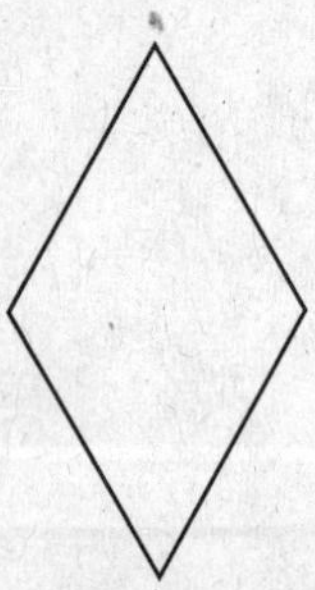

DIRECTIONS **1.** Color the object that is shaped like a circle. **2.** Which shape is a rectangle? Mark an X on that shape. **3.** Two of my shapes put together create a rhombus. What shape am I? Draw the shape.

School-Home Letter

Dear Family,

My class started Chapter 9 today. In the next few lessons, I will learn all about positions. I will also learn how to describe and copy different kinds of patterns.

Love, _____

Vocabulary

pattern a repeating design

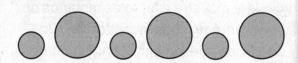

Home Activity

Grab a handful of change and ask your child to show you ways to make different patterns. Dimes and quarters can be put together to show patterns of size. Pennies and nickels can be put together to show patterns of color. See what other creative ways your child can come up with to show you different patterns!

Literature

Look for these books at the library. The colorful pictures and fun rhymes will help your child learn new and different patterns.

Pattern Fish by Trudy Harri. Millbrook Press, 2000.

Busy Bugs: A Book About Patterns by Jayne Harvey. Grosset & Dunlap, 2003.

Carta para la casa

Querida familia:

Mi clase comenzó hoy el Capítulo 9. En las próximas lecciones, aprenderé sobre las posiciones. También aprenderé a describir y copiar diferentes tipos de patrones.

Con cariño, _____

Vocabulario

patrón un diseño que se repite

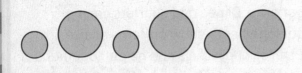

Actividad para la casa

Tome un puñado de cambio y pida a su hijo que le muestre diferentes maneras de formar patrones. Las monedas de 10¢ y de 25¢ se pueden juntar para mostrar patrones de tamaño. Las monedas de 1¢ y de 5¢ se pueden juntar para mostrar patrones de color. ¡Vea qué otras maneras creativas se le ocurren a su hijo para mostrar diferentes patrones!

Literatura

Busquen estos libros en la biblioteca. Las coloridas ilustraciones y las divertidas rimas ayudarán a su hijo a aprender patrones nuevos y diferentes.

Pattern Fish por Trudy Harri. Millbrook Press, 2000.

Busy Bugs: A Book About Patterns por Jayne Harvey. Grosset & Dunlap, 2003.

Name _____

Above, Below, Over, and Under

1

2

DIRECTIONS **1.** Place a red cube above the trees. Place a blue cube below the table. Draw and color the cubes. **2.** Place a red cube under the ball. Place a blue cube over the swing set. Draw and color the cubes.

Chapter 9

1

△ ◇ □ ◯
◯ ◯ ◯ ◯

Spiral Review

2

14
fourteen

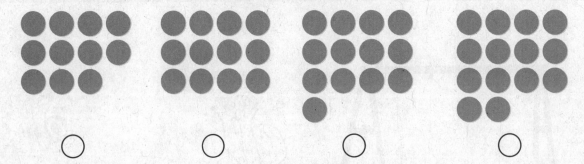

◯ ◯ ◯ ◯

3

five   six   seven   eight

◯ ◯ ◯ ◯

DIRECTIONS 1. Which shape is above the water bowl? Mark under your answer. **(Lesson 9.1) 2.** Which set has 14? Mark under your answer. **(Lesson 5.3) 3.** How many skateboards? Mark under your answer. **(Lesson 3.2)**

Name _____

Beside, Next To, and Between

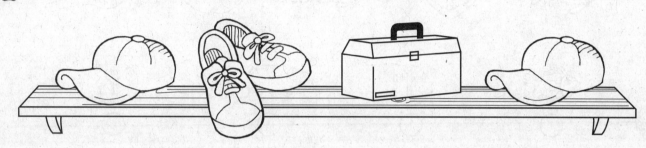

DIRECTIONS **1.** Place a cube on the cap that is beside the toolbox. Circle that cap. Place a cube on the cap that is next to the shoes. Mark an X on that cap. **2.** Place a cube on the football that is between two hats. Mark an X on that football. Place a cube on the football that is beside the skates. Circle that football. **3.** Place a cube on the watering can that is next to the shoes. Mark an X on that watering can.

Chapter 9

Lesson Check

◯　　　◯　　　◯　　　◯

Spiral Review

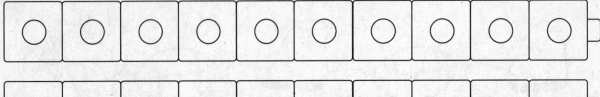

17　　　18　　　19　　　20

◯　　　◯　　　◯　　　◯

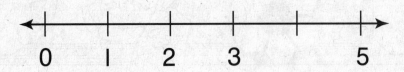

3　　　4　　　5　　　6

◯　　　◯　　　◯　　　◯

DIRECTIONS **1.** Which object is between the two fish? Mark under your answer. (Lesson 9.2) **2.** How many cubes? Mark under your answer. (Lesson 6.1) **3.** What number is missing from the number line? Mark under your answer. (Lesson 2.6)

Name _____

Algebra: Describe and Copy a Color Pattern

1

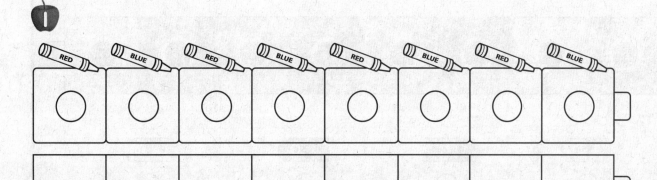

2

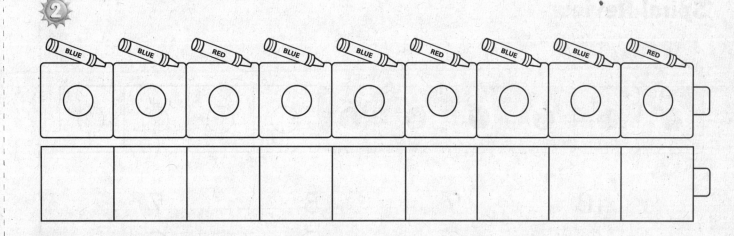

3

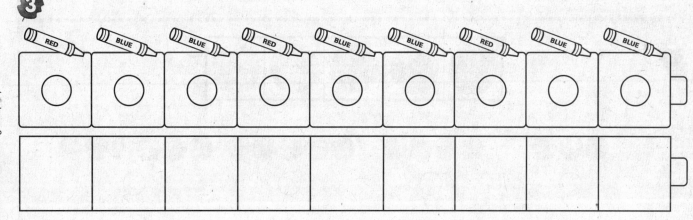

DIRECTIONS 1–3. Use red and blue crayons. Color the cubes in the top row to make a color pattern. Read to describe the pattern. Color the strip in the bottom row to copy the color pattern.

Chapter 9

Lesson Check

 1

○   ○   ○   ○

Spiral Review

2

  10   9   8   7

  ○   ○   ○   ○

3

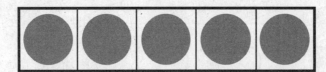

○   ○   ○   ○

DIRECTIONS **1.** Which set of cubes shows the color pattern? Mark under your answer. **(Lesson 9.3)** **2.** How many cubes in all? Mark under your answer. **(Lesson 4.2)** **3.** Count and tell how many counters are in the five frame. Mark under the set of counters that shows one fewer counter. **(Lesson 2.3)**

P198 one hundred ninety-eight

Name _____

Algebra: Describe and Copy a Shape Pattern

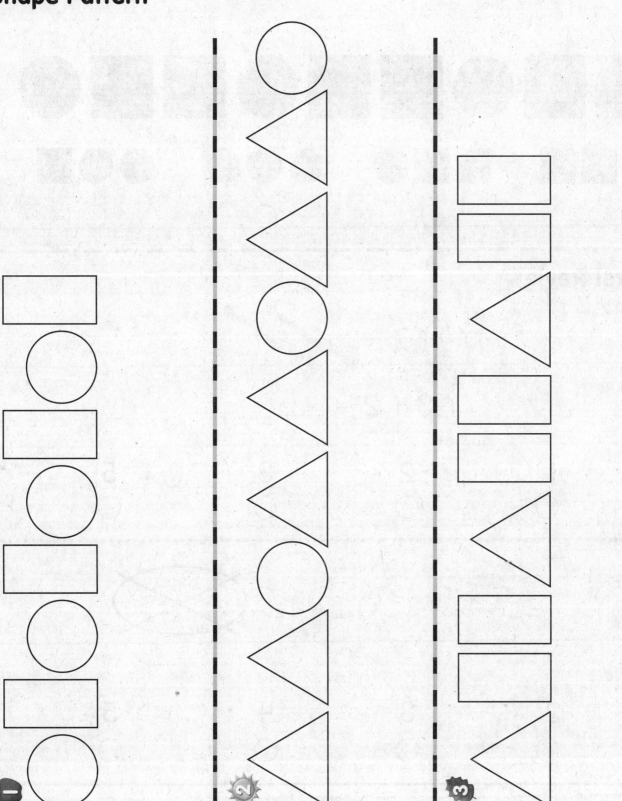

DIRECTIONS 1–3. Read to describe the pattern. Place shapes to copy the pattern. Draw and color the pattern.

Chapter 9

Lesson Check

○   ○   ○   ○

Spiral Review

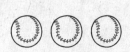   

$$3 + 2 = \underline{\quad}$$

1	2	3	5
○	○	○	○

2	3	4	5
○	○	○	○

DIRECTIONS **1.** Which set of shapes shows the pattern? Mark under your answer. (Lesson 9.4) **2.** How many objects in all? Mark under your answer. (Lesson 4.5) **3.** How many squirrels are left? Mark under your answer. (Lesson 4.10)

P200 two hundred

Name _____

Algebra: Describe and Copy a Size Pattern

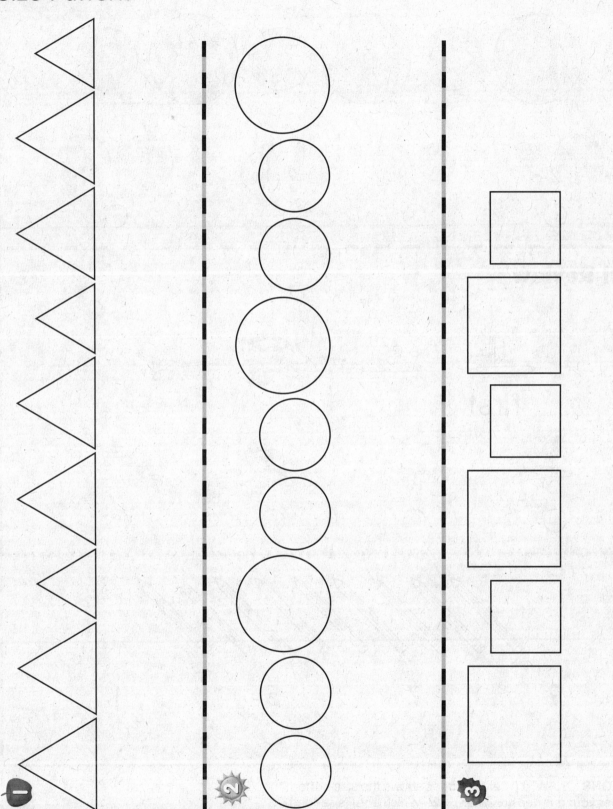

DIRECTIONS 1–3. Read to describe the pattern. Place shapes to copy the pattern. Draw and color the pattern.

Chapter 9

Lesson Check

◯ ◯ ◯ ◯

Sprial Review

first

   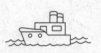

◯ ◯ ◯ ◯

9   7   5   1

◯ ◯ ◯ ◯

DIRECTIONS 1. Which set of shapes shows the size pattern?
Mark under your answer. **(Lesson 9.5)** 2. Which boat is second?
Mark under your answer. **(Lesson 2.7)** 3. How many pencils? Mark
under your answer. **(Lesson 3.7)**

Name _____

Find a Pattern • Number Patterns

 1
123 123 123

_____

- - - - - - - - - - - - - - - -

_____

2
121 121 121

_____

- - - - - - - - - - - - - - - -

_____

3
221 221 221

_____

- - - - - - - - - - - - - - - -

_____

DIRECTIONS   1–3. Read to describe the pattern. Write the numbers to copy the pattern. Which part of the pattern repeats again and again? Circle that part.

Lesson Check

1

2 1 2 2 1 2 2 1 2 2 1 2

1 1 1	2 1 2	2 2 2	1 2 3
○	○	○	○

Spiral Review

2

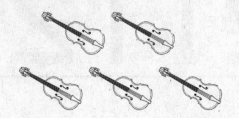   

$$5 + 3 = \underline{\hspace{1cm}}$$

10	8	5	3
○	○	○	○

3

7	8	9	10
○	○	○	○

DIRECTIONS **1.** Which set shows the part of the number pattern that repeats? Mark under your answer. **(Lesson 9.6)** **2.** Mark under your answer to show how many in all. **(Lesson 4.5)** **3.** How many umbrellas? Mark under your answer. **(Lesson 3.9)**

© Houghton Mifflin Harcourt Publishing Company

Name _____

Algebra: Extend a Shape Pattern

HANDS ON
Lesson 9.7

1 **2** 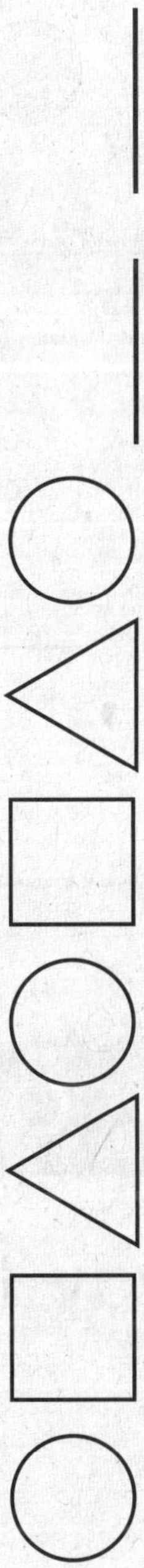 **3**

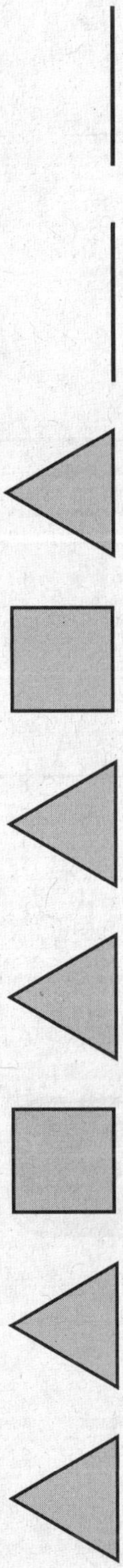

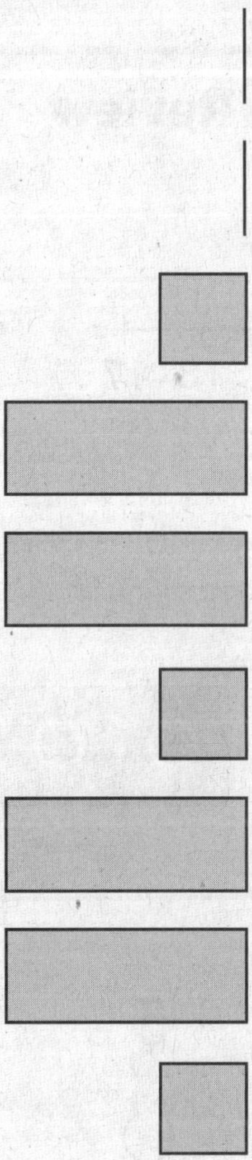

DIRECTIONS 1–3. Use shapes to copy the pattern. Place the two shapes that most likely come next. Draw and color the shapes.

Chapter 9

two hundred five **P205**

Lesson Check

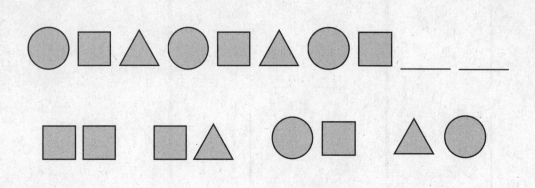

○   ○   ○   ○

Spiral Review

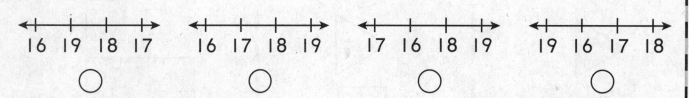

16 19 18 17	16 17 18 19	17 16 18 19	19 16 17 18
○	○	○	○

10 take away 1 is ___

5	9	10	11
○	○	○	○

DIRECTIONS 1. Which shapes are most likely come next in the shape pattern?
Mark under your answer. (Lesson 9.7) 2. Which number line shows the numbers
in the correct order? Mark under your answer. (Lesson 6.4) 3. How many are left?
Mark under your answer. (Lesson 4.10)

P206 two hundred six

Name _____

Algebra: Extend a Size Pattern

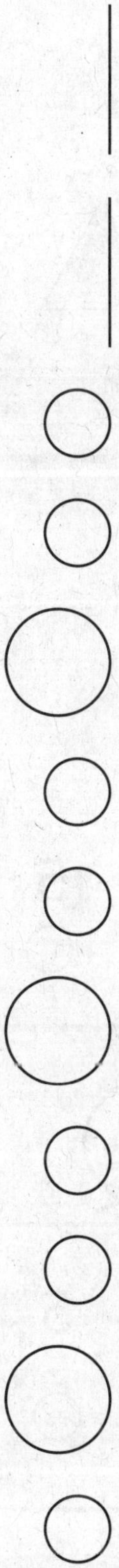

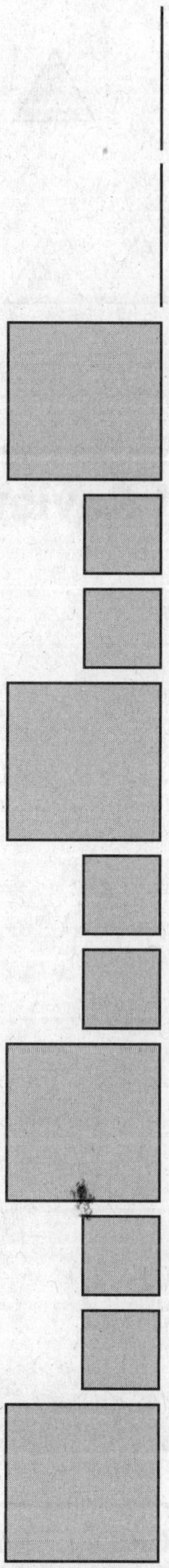

DIRECTIONS 1–3. Read to describe the size pattern. Which two shapes would most likely come next? Draw and color the shapes.

Chapter 9

two hundred seven **P207**

Lesson Check

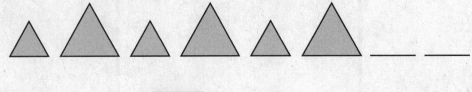

| ○ | ○ | ○ | ○ |

Spiral Review

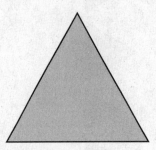

2	3	4	5
○	○	○	○

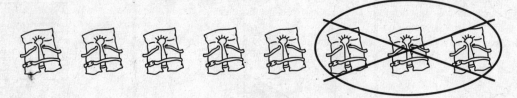

2	3	4	5
○	○	○	○

DIRECTIONS **1.** Which shapes are most likely come next in the size pattern? Mark under your answer. **(Lesson 9.8)** **2.** How many sides does the triangle have? Mark under your answer. **(Lesson 8.4)** **3.** How many life vests are left? Mark under your answer. **(Lesson 4.10)**

Algebra: Extend a Number Pattern

1

232323 __ __ __

2

311311311 __ __ __

3

343434 __ __ __

DIRECTIONS **1–3.** Look at the pattern. Which numbers are most likely to come next? Write the numbers to copy and extend the pattern.

Chapter 9

Lesson Check

①

322322322

1 2	2 2	3 2	3 4
○	○	○	○

Spiral Review

②

$$5 - 3 = \_\_\_$$

2	3	4	5
○	○	○	○

③

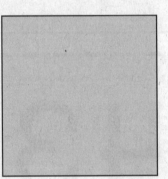

1	2	3	4
○	○	○	○

DIRECTIONS **1.** Which numbers are most likely to come next in the number pattern? Mark under your answer. **(Lesson 9.9)** **2.** How many lunch boxes are left? Mark under your answer. **(Lesson 4.12)** **3.** How many sides does the square have? Mark under your answer. **(Lesson 8.2)**

Name _____

Algebra: Describe and Copy a Growing Pattern

  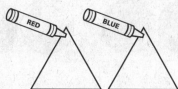 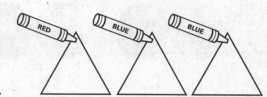

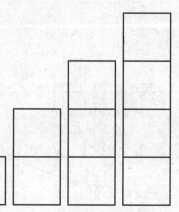

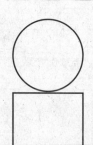 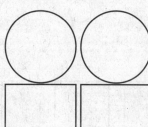 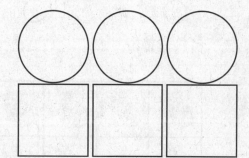

DIRECTIONS   1–3. Read to describe the pattern. Place shapes to copy the pattern. Draw and color the pattern.

Chapter 9

Lesson Check

Spiral Review

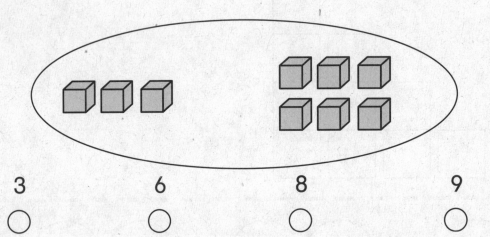

3   6   8   9
○   ○   ○   ○

17   18   19   20
○   ○   ○   ○

DIRECTIONS 1. Which pattern matches the growing pattern? Mark under your answer. **(Lesson 9.10)** 2. How many blocks in all? Mark under your answer. **(Lesson 4.3)** 3. How many pineapples? Mark under your answer. **(Lesson 6.1)**

Algebra: Create a Pattern

1

2

© Houghton Mifflin Harcourt Publishing Company

DIRECTIONS **I.** Use counters to make a pattern. Draw and color your pattern. Circle the part that repeats again and again. **2.** Use pattern blocks to make a pattern. Draw and color your pattern. Circle the part that repeats again and again.

Lesson Check

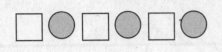

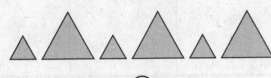

121212

Spiral Review

0   1   2   3
○   ○   ○   ○

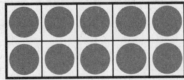
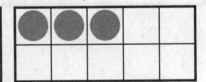

20   21   22   23
○   ○   ○   ○

DIRECTIONS **1.** Which pattern could you create from these counters? Mark under your answer. **(Lesson 9.11)** **2.** How many sides does the circle have? Mark under your answer. **(Lesson 8.6)** **3.** How many counters? Mark under your answer. **(Lesson 6.6)**

P214 two hundred fourteen

Chapter 9 Extra Practice

Lessons 9.1 – 9.3 (pp. 401 – 412) ·

1

2

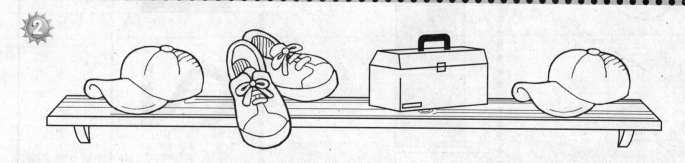

3

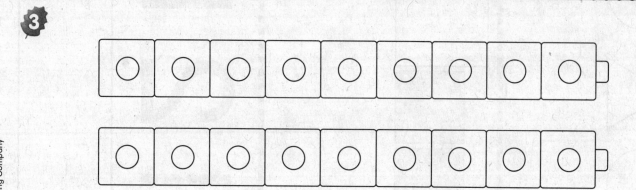

DIRECTIONS **1.** Place a red cube above the table. Place a blue cube below the table. Draw and color the cubes. **2.** Place a cube on the hat that is beside the shoes. Mark an X on that hat. **3.** Color the cubes in the top row to make a color pattern. Read to describe the pattern. Color the cubes in the bottom row to copy the color pattern.

1. △ ○ △ ○ △ ○ △ ○ △

2. □ ■ ■ □ ■ ■ □ ■ ■

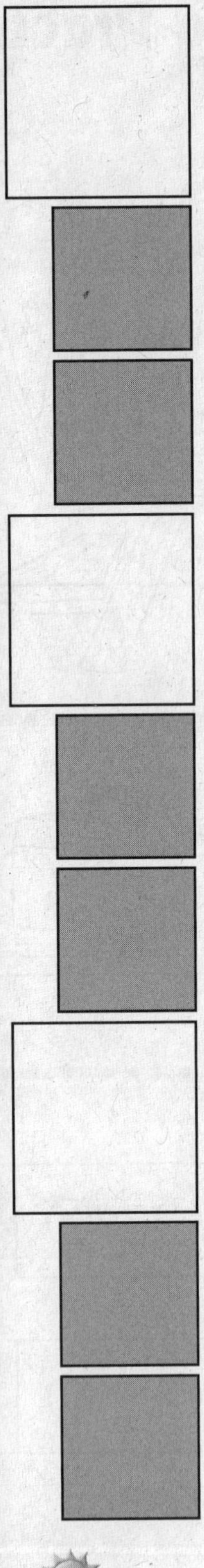

3. 2 1 2 1 2 1 2 1

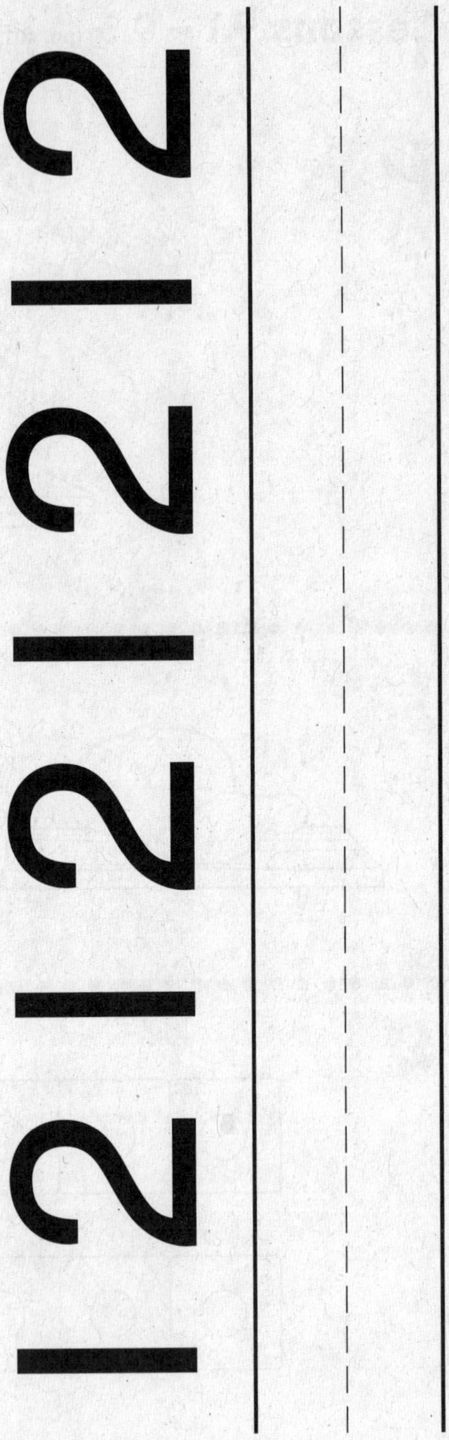

DIRECTIONS 1–2. Read to describe the pattern. Place shapes to copy the pattern. Draw and color the pattern.   3. Read to describe the pattern. Write to copy the pattern.

P216 two hundred sixteen

School-Home Letter

Dear Family,

My class started Chapter 10 today. In the next few lessons, I will learn about three-dimensional shapes. I will also learn how to sort by attributes.

Love, _____

Vocabulary

sphere a three-dimensional shape that is round
A ball is an example of a sphere.

cylinder a shape with a curved surface and two flat surfaces.

Home Activity

Take a walk around your neighborhood with your child. Look at the homes and buildings and ask your child to point out objects that are shaped like three-dimensional shapes.

Literature

Look for these books at the library. The photographs will help your child understand how shapes are a part of everyday life.

What in the World Is a Sphere? by Stuart J. Murphy. HarperCollins Publishers, 2001.

Cubes, Cones, Cylinders, & Spheres by Tana Hoban. Greenwillow, 2000.

Carta
para la casa

Querida familia:

Mi clase comenzó hoy el Capítulo 10. En las próximas lecciones, aprenderé sobre las figuras tridimensionales. También aprenderé a clasificar según los atributos.

Con cariño, _____

Vocabulario

esfera una figura tridimensional redonda. Una pelota es un ejemplo de una esfera.

cilindro una figura con una superficie curva y dos superficies planas.

Actividad para la casa

Salgan a caminar por su barrio. Observen las casas y los edificios y pida a su hijo que señale los objetos que tienen forma de figuras tridimensionales.

Literatura

Busquen estos libros en la biblioteca. Las fotografías ayudarán a su hijo a entender que las figuras son parte de la vida diaria.

What in the World Is a Sphere? por Stuart J. Murphy. HarperCollins Publishers, 2001.

Cubes, Cones, Cylinders, & Spheres por Tana Hoban. Greenwillow, 2000.

Identify and Describe Spheres

DIRECTIONS   Identify the objects that are shaped like a sphere. Mark an X on those objects.

Chapter 10

two hundred nineteen **P219**

Lesson Check

○   ○   ○   ○

Spiral Review

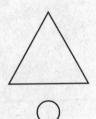 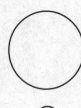 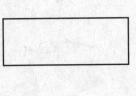 

○   ○   ○   ○

three   four   five   six

○   ○   ○   ○

DIRECTIONS   1. Which shape is a sphere? Mark under your answer.   (Lesson 10.1)
2. Which shape is a square? Mark under your answer.   (Lesson 8.1)
3. How many school buses? Mark under your answer.   (Lesson 3.2)

Identify and Describe Cubes

DIRECTIONS   Identify the objects that are shaped like a cube. Mark an X on those objects.

Lesson Check

Spiral Review

1   2   3   4

7   8   9   10

DIRECTIONS 1. Which shape is a cube? Mark under your answer. (Lesson 10.2)
2. How many sides does the square have? Mark under your answer.
(Lesson 8.2) 3. How many books in all? Mark under your answer. (Lesson 4.3)

P222 two hundred twenty-two

Identify and Describe Cylinders

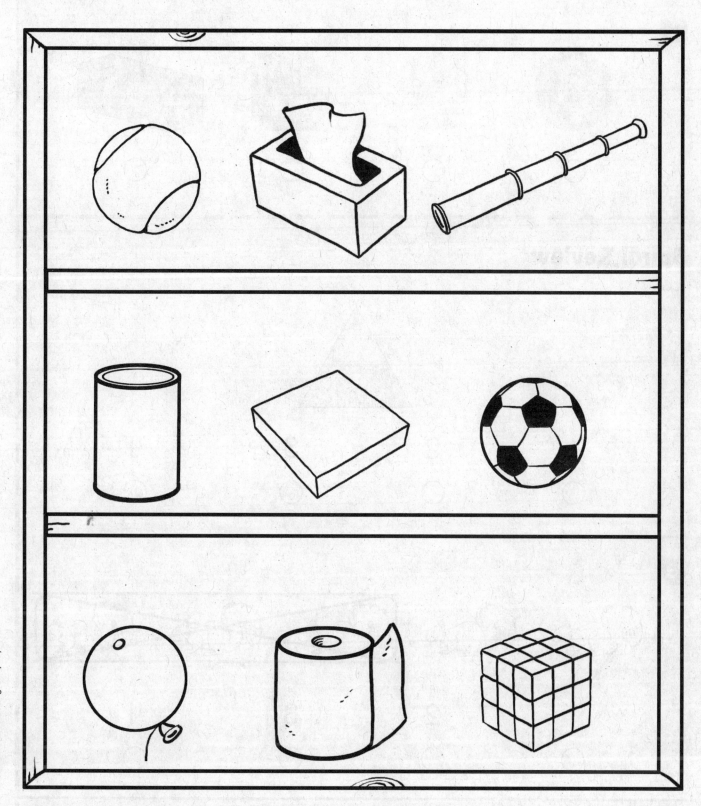

DIRECTIONS Identify the objects that are shaped like a cylinder.
Mark an X on those objects.

Chapter 10

Lesson Check

 1

○ ○ ○ ○

Spiral Review

2

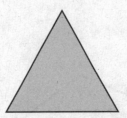

1   2   3   4

○ ○ ○ ○

3

1   2   3   4

○ ○ ○ ○

DIRECTIONS 1. Which shape is a cylinder? Mark under your answer. **(Lesson 10.3)**
2. How many sides does the triangle have? Mark under your answer. **(Lesson 8.4)**
3. How many squirrels are left? Mark under your answer. **(Lesson 4.10)**

Identify and Describe Cones

DIRECTIONS Identify the objects that are shaped like a cone. Mark an X on those objects.

Lesson Check

○　　　　　○　　　　　○　　　　　○

Spiral Review

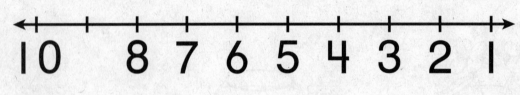

10　　8　7　6　5　4　3　2　1

8　　　　9　　　　　10　　　　　11

○　　　　○　　　　　○　　　　　○

five　　　six　　　seven　　　eight

○　　　　○　　　　　○　　　　　○

DIRECTIONS　1. Which shape is a cone? Mark under your answer.
(Lesson 10.4)　2. Which number is missing? Mark under your answer.
(Lesson 3.14)　3. How many dog houses? Mark under your answer.　(Lesson 3.4)

Identify and Describe Pyramids

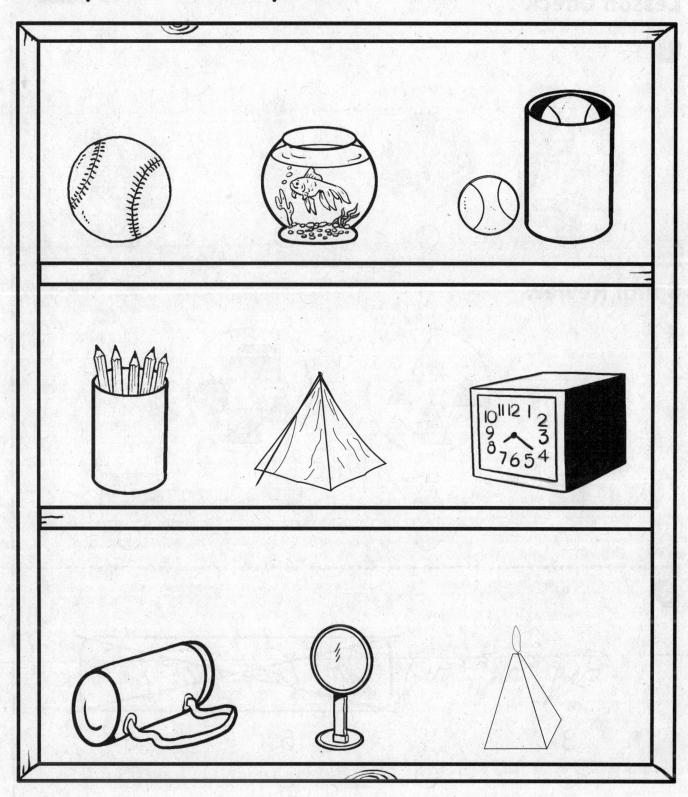

DIRECTIONS Identify the objects that are shaped like a pyramid.
Mark an X on those objects.

Lesson Check

○ ○ ○ ○

Spiral Review

 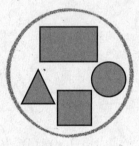

○ ○ ○ ○

3   4   5   6

○ ○ ○ ○

DIRECTIONS 1. Which shape is a pyramid? Mark under your answer. **(Lesson 10.5)** 2. Which shape is in both sorting rings? Mark under your answer. **(Lesson 7.2)** 3. How many dolphins are left? Mark under your answer. **(Lesson 4.9)**

Identify and Describe Rectangular Prisms

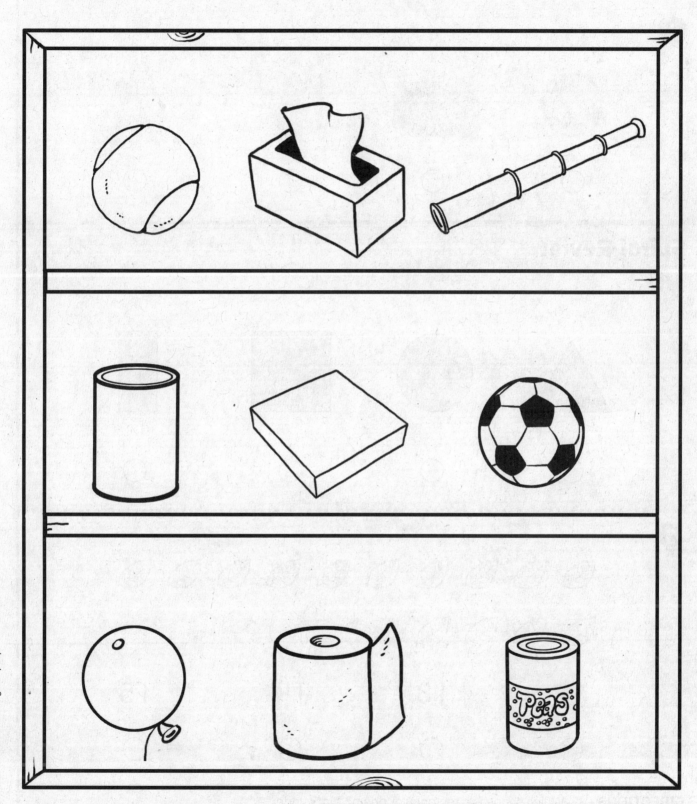

DIRECTIONS Identify the objects that are shaped like a rectangular prism. Mark an X on those objects.

Lesson Check

 1

Spiral Review

 2

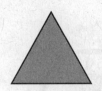

3

12   13   14   15

○   ○   ○   ○

DIRECTIONS   1. Which shape is a rectangular prism? Mark under your answer.   (Lesson 10.6)   2. Which shape has 3 sides? Mark under your answer.   (Lesson 8.4)   3. How many leaves? Mark under your answer.
(Lesson 5.3)

Draw a Picture • Sort Shapes

1.
roll

2.
stack

3.
slide

4.
stack and slide

DIRECTIONS   1. Which shape does not roll? Mark an X on that shape.   **2.** Which shape does not stack? Mark an X on that shape.   **3.** Which shape does not slide? Mark an X on that shape.   **4.** Which shape does not stack and slide? Mark an X on that shape.

Lesson Check

○　　○　　○　　○

Spiral Review

circle　　rectangle　　triangle　　square

○　　　○　　　○　　　○

12　　　11　　　8　　　6

○　　　○　　　○　　　○

DIRECTIONS 1. Which shape does not roll? Mark under your answer.
(Lesson 10.7)　2. Which shape does not belong? Mark under your answer.
(Lesson 7.3)　3. How many cubes? Mark under your answer. (Lesson 5.1)

P232 two hundred thirty-two

Chapter 10 Extra Practice

Lessons 10.1 – 10.2 (pp. 453 – 460) ·

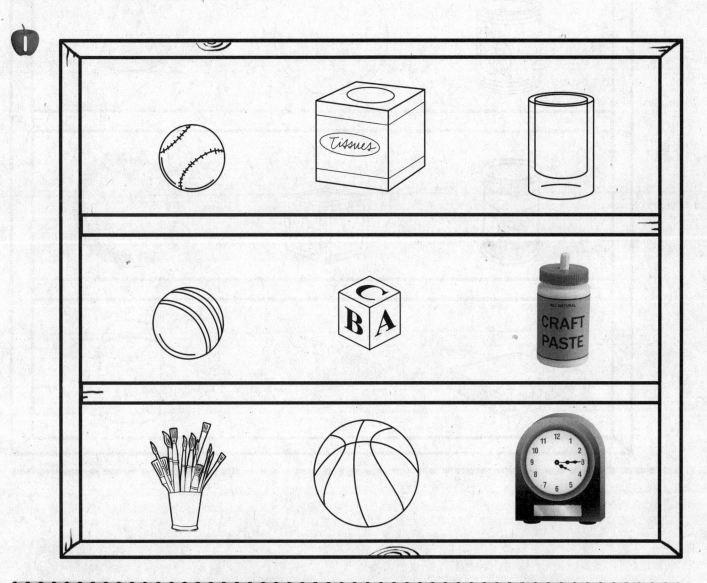

· ·

DIRECTIONS **1.** Identify the objects that are shaped like a sphere. Mark an X on those objects. Identify the objects that are shaped like a cube. Circle those objects. **2.** I have a curved surface. Which shape am I? Mark an X on that shape.

DIRECTIONS **1.** Identify the objects that are shaped like a cylinder. Mark an X on those objects. Identify the objects that are shaped like a cone. Circle those objects. **2.** Mark an X on the shape that is shaped like a rectangular prism. **3.** Circle the object that is shaped like a pyramid.

School-Home Letter

Dear Family,

My class started Chapter 11 today. In the next few lessons, I will learn about measurement. I will also learn how to compare and order objects according to their lengths, heights, and weights.

Love, _____

Vocabulary

longer than having a greater length compared to another object

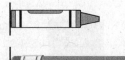

heavier having more weight compared to another object

Home Activity

Find 3 different-sized books. Ask your child to show you how to order them by lengths, heights, and weights.

Literature

Look for these books at the library. Each book will give you new ideas on how to enrich and encourage your child's measurement skills.

How Long or How Wide?: A Measuring Guide by Brian P. Cleary. Millbrook Press, 2007.

Measurement (Beginning Skills) by Amy DeCastro. Teacher Created Resources, 2004.

Carta
para la casa

Querida familia:

Mi clase comenzó hoy el Capítulo 11. En las próximas lecciones, aprenderé sobre la medición. También aprenderé a comparar y ordenar objetos según su longitud, altura y peso.

Con cariño, _____

Vocabulario

más largo que que tiene mayor longitud cuando se compara con otro objeto

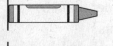

más pesado que tiene más peso cuando se compara con otro objeto

Actividad para la casa

Busque 3 libros de diferentes tamaños. Pida a su hijo que le muestre cómo ordenarlos según su longitud, altura y peso.

Literatura

Busquen estos libros en la biblioteca. Cada libro le proveerá nuevas ideas para ayudar a su hijo a reforzar las destrezas de medición.

How Long or How Wide?: A Measuring Guide por Brian P. Cleary. Millbrook Press, 2007.

Measurement (Begining Skills) por Amy DeCastro. Teacher Created Resources, 2004.

Compare Lengths

DIRECTIONS **1.** Make a cube train that is shorter. Draw the cube train.
2. Make a cube train that is longer. Draw the cube train. **3.** Make a cube
train that is about the same length. Draw the cube train.

Lesson Check

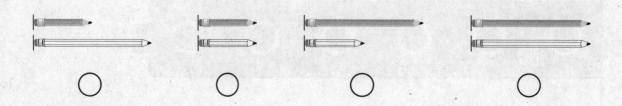

○   ○   ○   ○

Spiral Review

              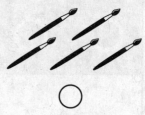

○   ○   ○   ○

7   8   9   10

○   ○   ○   ○

DIRECTIONS **1.** Which picture shows the gray pencil longer than the white pencil? Mark under your answer. **(Lesson 11.1)** **2.** How many paintbrushes? Compare the set in the five frame with the sets below. Mark under the set that shows fewer paintbrushes. **(Lesson 2.4)** **3.** How many bowling pins? Mark under your answer. **(Lesson 3.9)**

Order Lengths

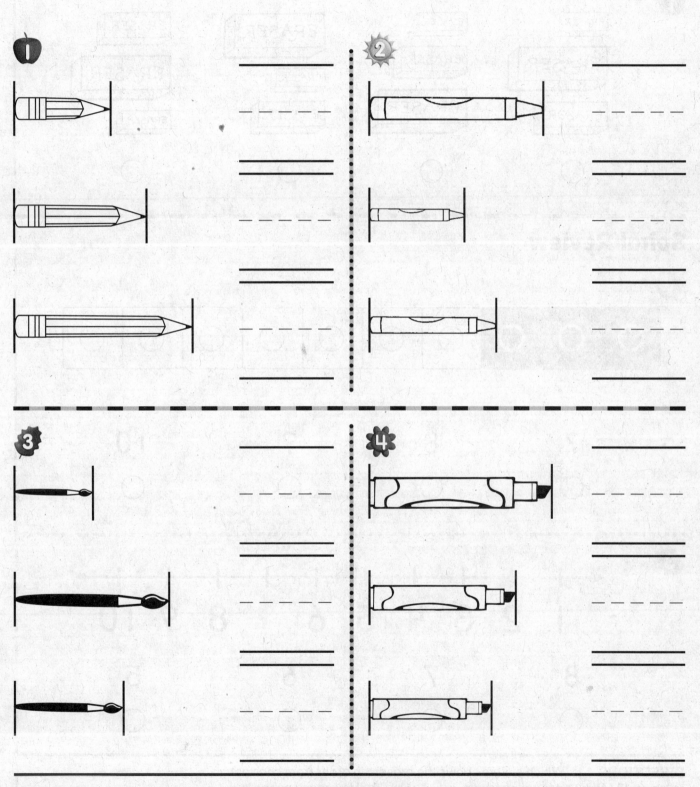

DIRECTIONS 1–4. Write the numbers *1, 2,* and *3* to order the objects from shortest to longest.

Lesson Check

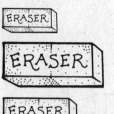  

◯   ◯   ◯   ◯

Spiral Review

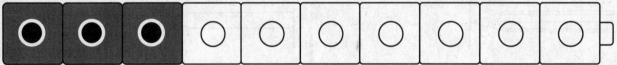

7   8   9   10
◯   ◯   ◯   ◯

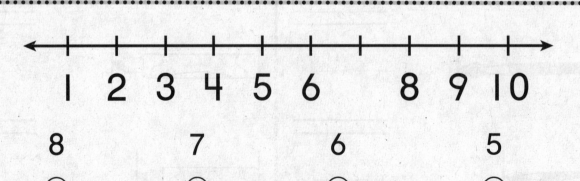

8   7   6   5
◯   ◯   ◯   ◯

DIRECTIONS **1.** Which picture shows the erasers in order from shortest to longest? Mark under your answer. **(Lesson 11.2)** **2.** How many cubes in all? Mark under your answer. **(Lesson 4.2)** **3.** Begin with 1. Count forward. What is the missing number? Mark under your answer. **(Lesson 3.13)**

Name _____

Compare Lengths Using Nonstandard Units

 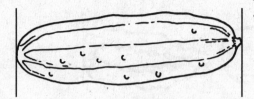

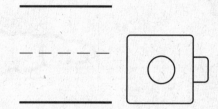

 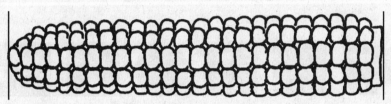

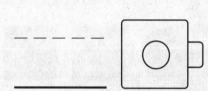

 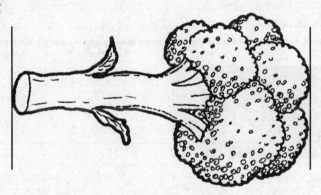

DIRECTIONS   1–3. Use a cube train to measure how long the vegetable is. Draw the cube train. Write about how many cubes long it is. Mark an X on the shortest vegetable. Circle the longest vegetable.

Chapter 11

two hundred forty-one **P241**

Lesson Check

1

3   4   5   6

○   ○   ○   ○

Spiral Review

2

○   ○   ○   ○

3

1   2   3   4

○   ○   ○   ○

DIRECTIONS **1.** About how many cubes long is the carrot? Mark under your answer. **(Lesson 11.3)** **2.** Which shapes most likely come next in the pattern? Mark under your answer. **(Lesson 9.9)** **3.** How many sides does a rectangle have? Mark under your answer. **(Lesson 8.7)**

Name _____

Compare Heights

DIRECTIONS Find two crayons of different heights. Place the crayons on the line and compare the heights. Draw the crayons. Circle the taller crayon. Mark an X on the shorter crayon.

Chapter 11

Lesson Check

○　　　　○　　　　○　　　　○

Spiral Review

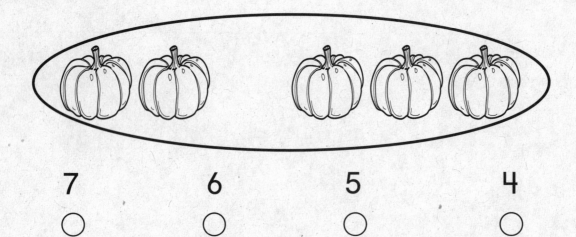

7　　　　6　　　　5　　　　4

○　　　　○　　　　○　　　　○

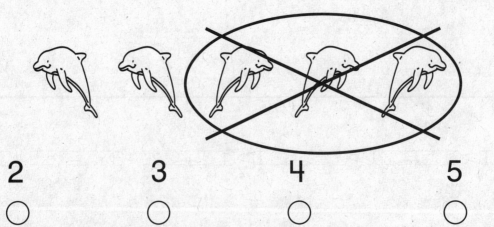

2　　　　3　　　　4　　　　5

○　　　　○　　　　○　　　　○

DIRECTIONS **1.** Which picture shows the flower that is taller than the pot? Mark under your answer. **(Lesson 11.4)** **2.** How many pumpkins in all? Mark under your answer. **(Lesson 4.3)** **3.** How many dolphins are left? Mark under your answer. **(Lesson 4.10)**

Draw a Picture • Order Heights

_____   _____

- -

_____   _____

DIRECTIONS   1. This is the tallest of 3 plants in order from tallest to shortest. Draw to show the other 2 plants.   **2.** This is the shortest of 3 flowers in order from shortest to tallest. Draw to show the other 2 flowers.

Lesson Check

○ ○ ○ ○

Spiral Review

$$8 - 3 = \underline{\hspace{1cm}}$$

2   3   4   5

○   ○   ○   ○

 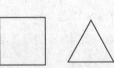 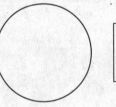

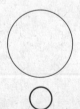

○   ○   ○   ○

DIRECTIONS   **1.** Which cube tower is the shortest? Mark under your answer.
(Lesson 11.5)   **2.** How many bananas are left? Mark under your answer.
(Lesson 4.12)   **3.** Which object does not belong? Mark under your answer.   (Lesson 7.3)

P246   two hundred forty-six

Name _____

Compare and Order Weights

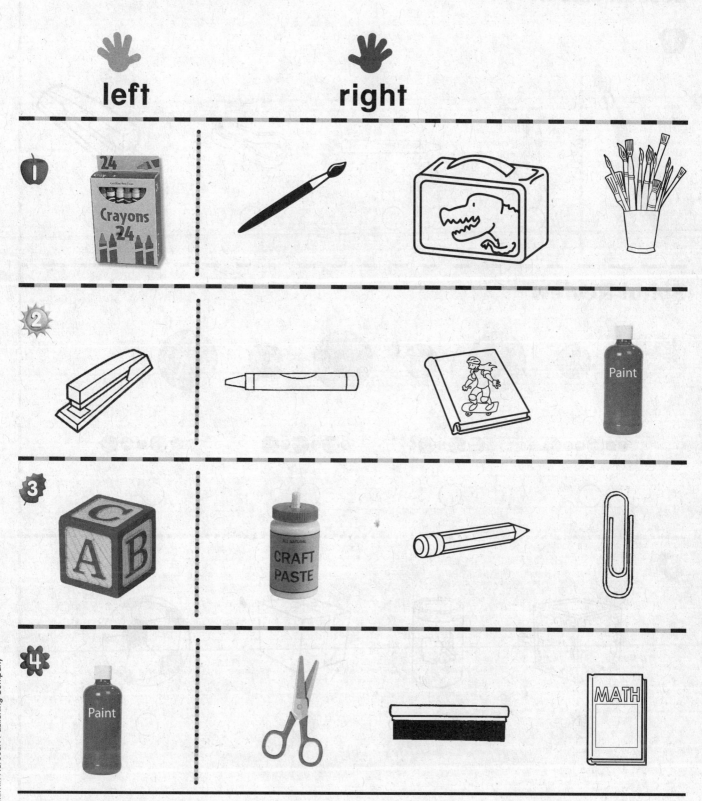

left   right

1.

2.

3.

4.

DIRECTIONS Find the first object in the row, and hold it in your left hand. Find the rest of the objects in the row, and hold each object in your right hand. **1–2.** Circle the object that is lighter than the object in your left hand. **3–4.** Circle the object that is heavier than the object in your left hand.

Lesson Check

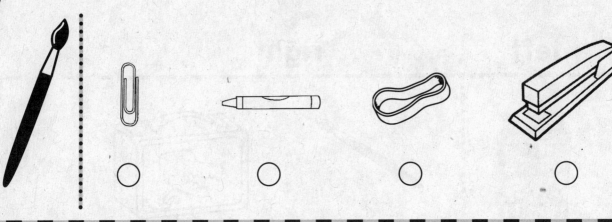

○　　　　○　　　　○　　　　○

Spiral Review

○　　　　○　　　　○　　　　○

○　　　　○　　　　○　　　　○

DIRECTIONS **I.** Which object is heavier than the paintbrush? Mark under your answer. (Lesson 11.6) **2.** Identify the pattern. Which pattern is the same? Mark under your answer. (Lesson 9.5) **3.** Which object is shaped like a cylinder? Mark under your answer. (Lesson 10.3)

Length, Height, and Weight

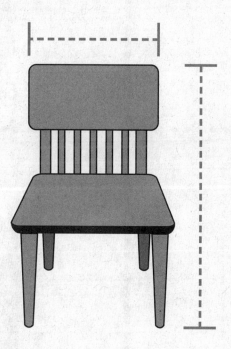

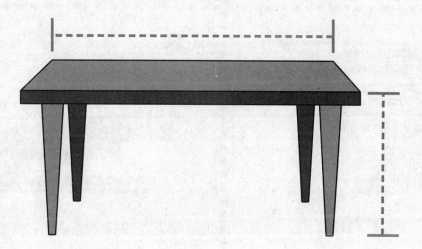

DIRECTIONS   1–2. Use red to trace the line that shows how long the object is. Use blue to trace the line that shows how tall the object is. Talk about another way to measure the object.

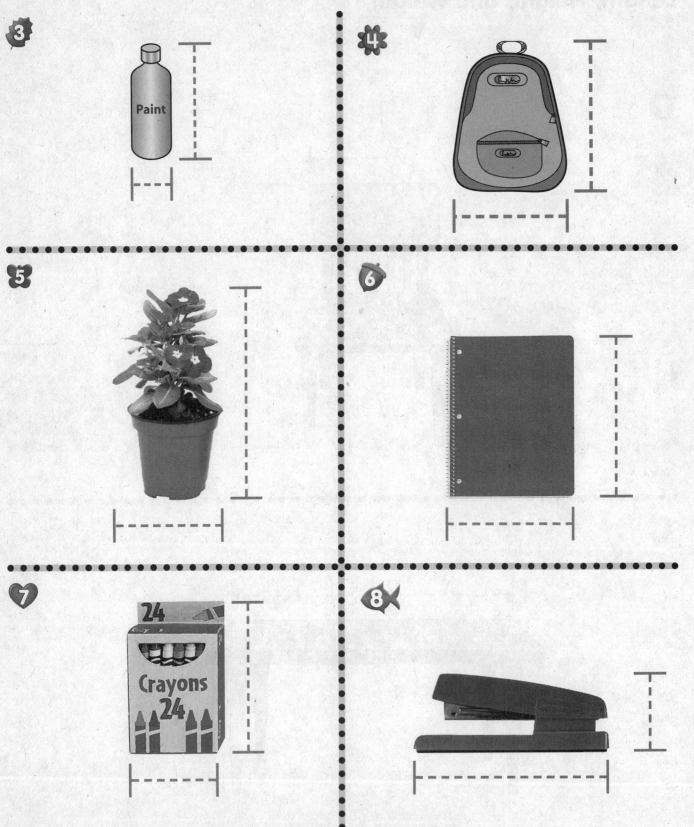

3

Paint

4

5

6

7

Crayons
24

8

DIRECTIONS 3–8. Use red to trace the line that shows how long the object is. Use blue to trace the line that shows how tall the object is. Talk about another way to measure the object.

P248b Two hundred forty-eight

Name _____

Hands On: Explore Capacity

about 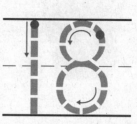 handfuls

---

1

about _____ handfuls

2

about _____ handfuls

3

about _____ handfuls

DIRECTIONS 1–3. Use drinking cups like the cups pictured. Fill each cup with handfuls of rice. Write about how many handfuls each cup holds.

Chapter 11

two hundred forty-eight **P248c**

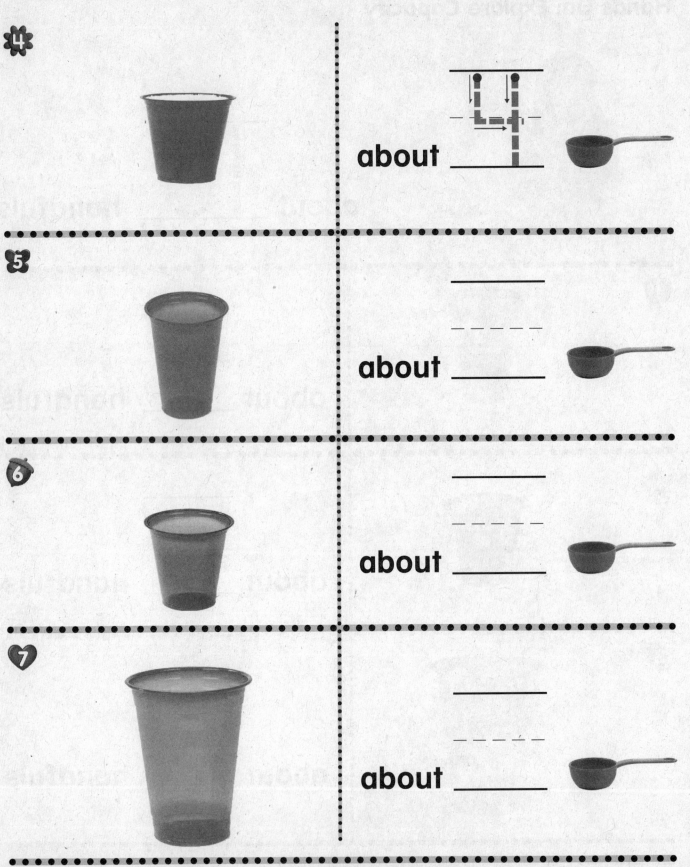

4 about _____

5 _____
about _____

6 _____
about _____

7 _____
about _____

DIRECTIONS **4–7.** Use drinking cups like the cups pictured. Fill each cup with scoops of rice. Write about how many scoops each cup holds.

Name _____

Chapter 11 Extra Practice

Lessons 11.1 – 11.2 (pp. 497 – 504) ·

1

2

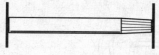
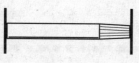
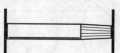

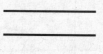

DIRECTIONS   1. Make a cube train that is about the same length. Draw the cube train.   **2.** Write the numbers *1*, *2*, and *3* to order the objects from shortest to longest.

2

3

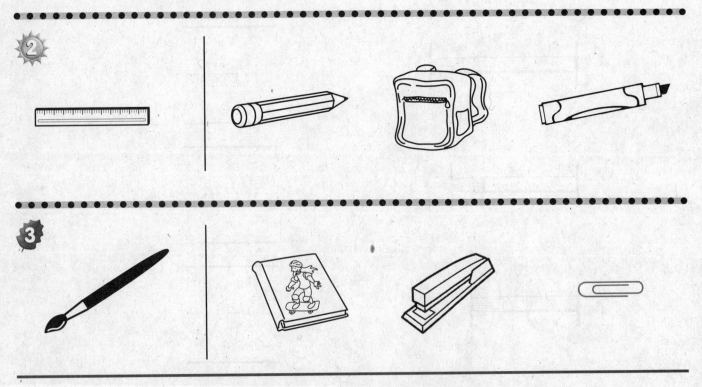

DIRECTIONS **1.** Find 3 classroom objects that have different heights. Draw the objects in order from shortest to tallest. **2–3.** Find the first object in the row, and hold it in your left hand. Find the rest of the objects in the row, and hold each object in your right hand. **2.** Circle the object that is heavier than the object in your left hand. **3.** Circle the object that is lighter than the object in your left hand.

School-Home
Letter

Dear Family,

My class started Chapter 12 today. In the next few lessons, I will learn about money. I will identify pennies, nickels, dimes, and quarters and learn the value of each.

Love, _____

Vocabulary

penny, nickel, dime, quarter

Coins with the value of one cent, five cents, ten cents, and twenty-five cents, respectively.

Home Activity

Help your child sort, identify, and compare different coins. Help your child trade 5 pennies for 1 nickel.

Literature

Look for these books at the library. These books have beautiful illustrations and clever stories that will keep your child interested in learning more about money.

Bunny Money by Rosemary Wells. Puffin, 2000.

The Berenstain Bears' Trouble with Money by Stan and Jan Berenstain. Random House, 1983.

Carta
para la casa

Querida familia:

Mi clase comenzó hoy el Capítulo 12. En las próximas lecciones, aprenderé sobre el dinero. Aprenderé a identificar monedas de 1, 5, 10 y 25 centavos, y cuánto valen.

Con cariño, _____

Vocabulario

monedas de 1, 5, 10 y 25 centavos

Actividad para la casa

Ayude a su hijo a ordenar, identificar y comparar distintas monedas. Ayúdelo a cambiar 5 monedas de 1 centavo por una moneda de 5 centavos.

Literatura

Busquen estos libros en la biblioteca. Las coloridas ilustraciones e imaginativas historias mantendrán a su hijo interesado en aprender más sobre el dinero.

Bunny Money
por Rosemary Wells.
Puffin, 2000.

The Berenstain Bears' Trouble with Money
por Stan y Jan Berenstain.
Random House, 1983.

Name _____

Penny

_____ cent

_____ cent

_____ cents

_____ cents

_____ cents

_____ cents

DIRECTIONS **1.** Trace the number that shows the value of the coin. **2–6.** Count the pennies. Write how many cents.

2 cents   3 cents   4 cents   5 cents

◯   ◯   ◯   ◯

Spiral Review

◯   ◯   ◯   ◯

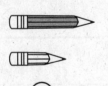 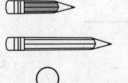 

◯   ◯   ◯   ◯

DIRECTIONS **I.** Count the pennies. How many cents? Mark under your answer.
(Lesson 12.1) **2.** What shape is the orange? Mark under your answer.
(Lesson 10.1) **3.** Which picture shows a gray pencil that is shorter than a white pencil?
Mark under your answer. **(Lesson 11.1)**

Name _____

Nickel

5 cents

_____ cents

_____

_____ cents

_____

_____ cents

5¢

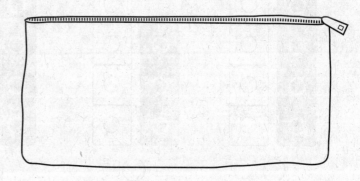

DIRECTIONS 1. Trace the number that shows the value of the coin. **2–4.** Write how many cents. Circle the coin or set of coins that shows 5 cents. **5.** Place the coin or coins on the workspace that are needed to buy the toy. Draw the coins.

Lesson Check

1 cent	5 cents	10 cents	25 cents
○	○	○	○

Spiral Review

1	2	3	4
○	○	○	○

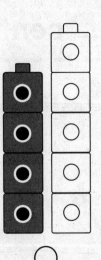 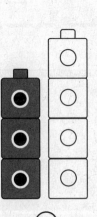 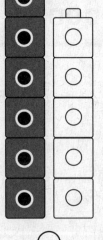 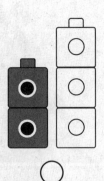

○   ○   ○   ○

DIRECTIONS **1.** Which shows the value of the coin? Mark under your answer.
(Lesson 12.2) **2.** How many vertices does the square have? Mark under your answer.
(Lesson 8.2) **3.** Which picture shows the gray cube tower that is taller than the white cube tower? Mark under your answer. **(Lesson 11.4)**

Name _____

Dime

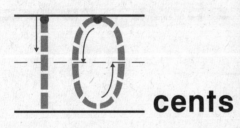

_____ cents

_____ cents

3

_____ _____ cents

4

_____ _____ cents

DIRECTIONS **1.** Trace the number that shows the value of the coin. **2–4.** Write how many cents. Circle the coin or set of coins that shows 10 cents.

Lesson Check

1 cent	5 cents	10 cents	25 cents
○	○	○	○

Spiral Review

○   ○   ○   ○

○   ○   ○   ○

DIRECTIONS **1.** Which number shows the value of the coin? Mark under your answer. **(Lesson 12.3)** **2.** Which object is heavier than the book? Mark under your answer. **(Lesson 11.6)** **3.** Which shape is a cube? Mark under your answer. **(Lesson 10.2)**

Name _____

Quarter

 **cents**

- - - - - - - - - - - - - - - - - - - -

_____
- - - - -
_____ **cents**

DIRECTIONS **1.** Trace the number that shows the value of the coin. **2.** Write how many cents. Circle the coin or set of coins that shows 25 cents.

Chapter 12

I cent   5 cents   10 cents   25 cents
○   ○   ○   ○

Spiral Review

○   ○   ○   ○

17

○   ○   ○   ○

DIRECTIONS **1.** Which shows the value of the coin? Mark under your answer. **(Lesson 12.4)** **2.** Which object is shaped like a sphere? Mark under your answer. **(Lesson 10.1)** **3.** Which ten frame shows 17? Mark under your answer. **(Lesson 5.7)**

Name _____

Draw a Picture • Use Coins

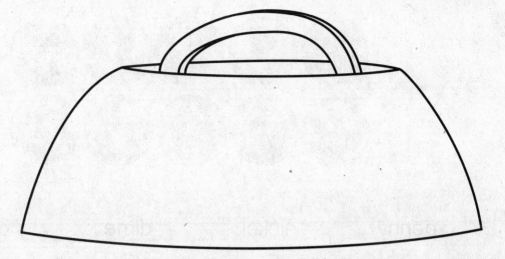

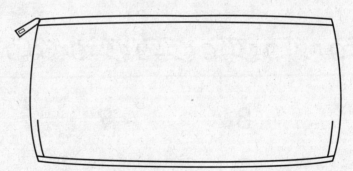

DIRECTIONS 1. How can you use pennies to show the value of the coin? Draw and color the pennies. 2. How can you use one nickel and some pennies to show the value of the coin? Draw and color the coins. 3. How can you use nickels to show the value of the coin? Draw and color the nickels.

Chapter 12

Lesson Check

1

penny	nickel	dime	quarter
○	○	○	○

Spiral Review

2

1	2	3	0
○	○	○	○

3

7	8	9	10
○	○	○	○

DIRECTIONS 1. Which coin shows the value of the set of coins above? Mark under your answer. **(Lesson 12.5) 2.** How many straight sides does a circle have? Mark under your answer. **(Lesson 8.5) 3.** How many caterpillars? Mark under your answer. **(Lesson 3.7)**

Chapter 12 Extra Practice

Lessons 12.1 – 12.2 (pp. 529 – 535) · · · · · · · · · · · · · · · · · ·

_____

- - - - - - -

———— cent

_____

- - - - - - -

———— cents

_____

- - - - - - -

———— cents

_____

- - - - - - -

———— cents

DIRECTIONS 1–2. Count the pennies. Write how many cents.
3–4. Write how many cents. Circle the coin or set of coins that shows 5 cents.

Chapter 12   two hundred sixty-three **P263**

1

_____

- - - - - - - - - -

_____ **cents**

2

_____

- - - - - - - - - -

_____ **cents**

3

DIRECTIONS **1.** Write how many cents. Circle the coin that shows 25 cents. Mark an X on the coin that shows 10 cents. **3.** How can you use 1 nickel and some pennies to show the value of the coin? Draw and color the coins.

Name _____

Add One

1  +  ==

2

2 + _____ == _____

3

3 + _____ == _____

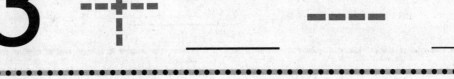

4

4 + _____ == _____

DIRECTIONS **1.** Place cubes as shown above the numbers.
Trace the cubes. Trace to complete the addition sentence.
2–4. Use cubes to show the number. Draw the cubes.
Show and draw one more cube. Complete the addition sentence.

Getting Ready for Grade 1

$5 \; + \; \text{-----} \; = \; \text{-----}$

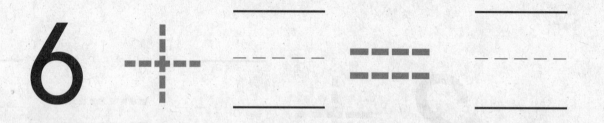

$6 \; + \; \text{-----} \; = \; \text{-----}$

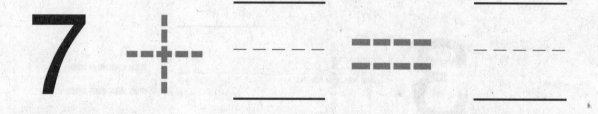

$7 \; + \; \text{-----} \; = \; \text{-----}$

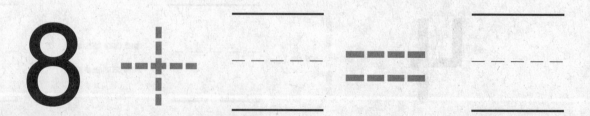

$8 \; + \; \text{-----} \; = \; \text{-----}$

DIRECTIONS 5–8. Use cubes to show the number. Draw the cubes. Show and draw one more cube. Complete the addition sentence.

HOME ACTIVITY • Show your child a set of one to nine pennies. Have him or her use pennies to show how to add one to the set. Then have him or her tell how many in all.

Add Two

1

2

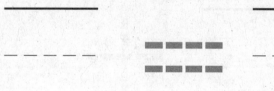

3

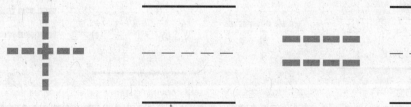

DIRECTIONS 1. Count how many shells on the left. Trace the two shells being added. Trace to complete the addition sentence. **2–3.** Count how many shells. Write the number. Draw two more shells. Complete the addition sentence.

4

_____   +   - - - - - -   ===   _____

5

_____   +   - - - - - -   ===   _____

6

_____   +   - - - - - -   ===   _____

DIRECTIONS 4–6. Count how many shells. Write the number. Draw two more shells. Complete the addition sentence.

HOME ACTIVITY • Draw objects in a column beginning with a set of 1 to a set of 8. Have your child draw two more objects beside each set, and write how many in all.

P268 two hundred sixty-eight

Add on a Ten Frame

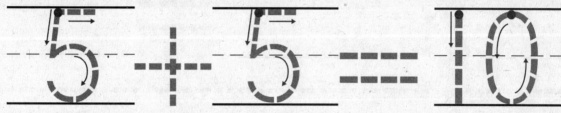

red	red	red	red	red
yellow	yellow	yellow	yellow	yellow

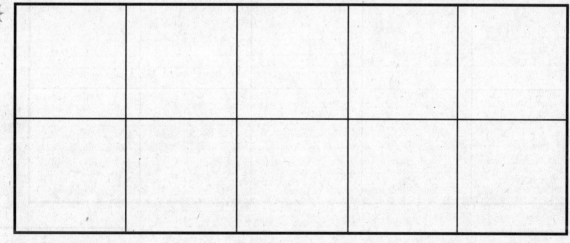

© Houghton Mifflin Harcourt Publishing Company

DIRECTIONS **1.** Place counters on the ten frame as shown.
Trace the addition sentence. **2.** Place some counters red side up
on the ten frame. Add more counters yellow side up to fill the ten
frame. Complete the addition sentence.

Getting Ready for Grade 1

two hundred sixty-nine **P269**

3

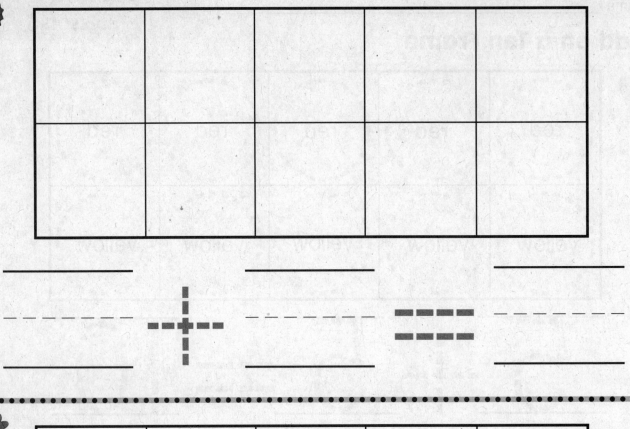

_____   _____   _____

- - - - - - - ➕ - - - - - - - 🟰 - - - - - - -

_____   _____   _____

4

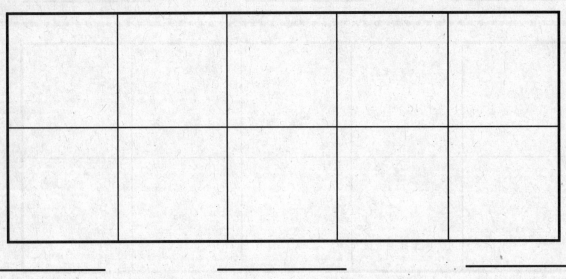

_____   _____   _____

- - - - - - - ➕ - - - - - - - 🟰 - - - - - - -

_____   _____   _____

DIRECTIONS 3–4. Place a different number of counters red side up on the ten frame. Add more counters yellow side up to fill the ten frame. Complete the addition sentence.

HOME ACTIVITY • Give your child some household objects, such as two different kinds of buttons. Have your child arrange the buttons to show different ways to make 10, such as 6 red buttons and 4 blue buttons. Write the addition sentence.

Part-Part-Whole

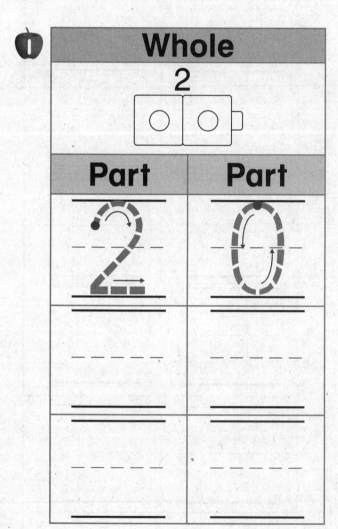

DIRECTIONS 1–2. How many cubes in all? Place that many cubes in the workspace. Show the different parts that make the whole. Complete the chart to show all the parts that make the whole.

Getting Ready for Grade 1

two hundred seventy-one **P271**

Whole	
4	

Part	**Part**
——————	——————
- - - -	- - - -
═══════	═══════
═══════	═══════
- - - -	- - - -
═══════	═══════
═══════	═══════
- - - -	- - - -
═══════	═══════
═══════	═══════
- - - -	- - - -
═══════	═══════
═══════	═══════
- - - -	- - - -
═══════	═══════

Whole	
5	

Part	**Part**
——————	——————
- - - -	- - - -
═══════	═══════
═══════	═══════
- - - -	- - - -
═══════	═══════
═══════	═══════
- - - -	- - - -
═══════	═══════
═══════	═══════
- - - -	- - - -
═══════	═══════
═══════	═══════
- - - -	- - - -
═══════	═══════
═══════	═══════
- - - -	- - - -
═══════	═══════

DIRECTIONS   3–4. How many cubes in all? Complete the chart to show all the parts that make the whole.

HOME ACTIVITY • Have your child use buttons or macaroni pieces to show the different parts that make the whole set of 8 (e.g. 7 and 1, 6 and 2, 5 and 3, 4 and 4 etc.)

© Houghton Mifflin Harcourt Publishing Company

Name _____

Addition Sentences

 1

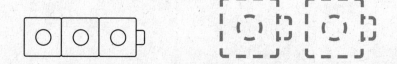

$3 + 2 = 5$

 2

$4 + \underline{} = 7$

 3

$6 + \underline{} = 10$

DIRECTIONS **1.** How many cubes are being added? Trace the cubes. Trace to complete the addition sentence. **2–3.** What number is missing in the addition sentence? Draw cubes to show that number. Write the number to complete the addition sentence.

Getting Ready for Grade 1   two hundred seventy-three **P273**

4

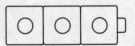

$$3 + \underline{} = 8$$

5

$$5 + \underline{} = 6$$

6

$$5 + \underline{} = 10$$

DIRECTIONS 4–6. What number is missing in the addition sentence? Draw cubes to show that number. Write the number to complete the addition sentence.

HOME ACTIVITY • Use self-stick notes or small pieces of paper to write addition sentences as shown above. Have your child fill in the missing number to complete each addition sentence.

Name _____

 **Checkpoint**

Concepts and Skills

$$9 + \underline{} = \underline{}$$

$$\underline{} + \underline{} = \underline{}$$

DIRECTIONS 1. Use cubes to show the number. Draw the cubes. Show and draw one more cube. Complete the addition sentence. **(pp. P265–P266) 2.** Place some counters red side up on the ten frame. Add more counters yellow side up to fill the ten frame. Complete the addition sentence. **(pp. P269–P270)**

Getting Ready for Grade 1   two hundred seventy-five **P275**

3

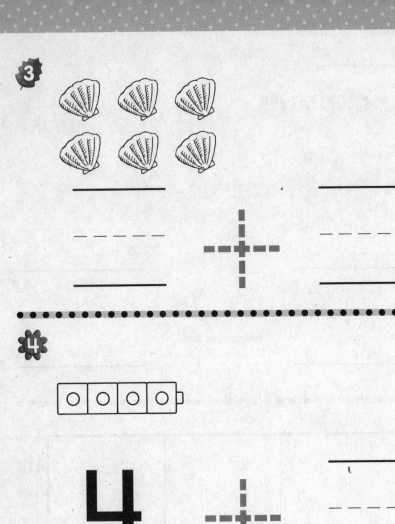

_____   +   _____   =   _____

- - - - - - -

· ·

4

$$4 \quad + \quad \underline{\hspace{2cm}} \quad = \quad 8$$

· ·

5

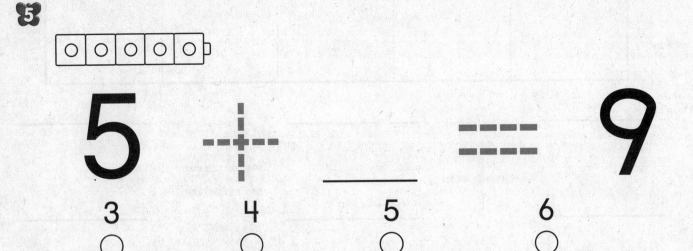

$$5 \quad + \quad \underline{\hspace{2cm}} \quad = \quad 9$$

  3   4   5   6

  ◯   ◯   ◯   ◯

DIRECTIONS **3.** Count how many shells. Write the number. Draw two more shells. Complete the addition sentence. (pp. P267–P268) **4.** What number is missing in the addition sentence? Draw cubes to show that number. Write the number to complete the addition sentence. (pp. P273–P274) **5.** Mark under the number that is missing in the addition sentence. (pp. P273–P274)

Name _____

Subtract One

1

$10 - 1 = 9$

2

9 − ___ = ___

3

8 − ___ = ___

DIRECTIONS 1. Place cubes on the ones shown. Trace the cubes. Trace the circle and X on the cube being taken away. Trace to complete the subtraction sentence. **2–3.** Use cubes to show the number. Draw the cubes. Take away one cube. Circle the cube that you took away and mark an X on it. Complete the subtraction sentence.

Getting Ready for Grade 1 two hundred seventy-seven **P277**

4

7 ---- _____ ____ === _____
              ____   _____

5

6 ---- _____ ==== _____
              ____   _____

6

5 ---- _____ === _____
              ____   _____

DIRECTIONS 4–6. Use cubes to show the number. Draw the cubes. Take away one cube. Circle the cube that you took away and mark an X on it. Complete the subtraction sentence.

HOME ACTIVITY • Ask your child to use toys to demonstrate and describe the number pattern in the subtraction sentences on this page.

Subtract Two

$$3 - 2 = 1$$

_____ _____ _____

- - -   = = =   - - -

_____ _____ _____

_____ _____ _____

- - -   = = =   - - -

_____ _____ _____

DIRECTIONS 1. Count how many boats in all. Trace the circle and the X that shows the boats that sail away. Trace to complete the subtraction sentence. **2–3.** Count how many boats in all. Write the number. Two boats sail away. Circle the boats that sail away. Mark an X on them. Complete the subtraction sentence.

© Houghton Mifflin Harcourt Publishing Company

Getting Ready for Grade 1

4

_____ 　 - - - - _____ ▮▮▮▮ _____

- - - -　▮▮▮▮　- - - -　▮▮▮▮　- - - -

_____ 　 _____ 　 _____

5

_____ 　 _____ 　 _____

- - - -　▮▮▮▮　- - - -　▮▮▮▮　- - - -

_____ 　 _____ 　 _____

6

_____ 　 _____ 　 _____

- - - -　▮▮▮▮　- - - -　▮▮▮▮　- - - -

_____ 　 _____ 　 _____

DIRECTIONS 4–6. Count how many boats in all. Write the number. Two boats sail away. Circle the boats that sail away. Mark an X on them. Complete the addition sentence.

HOME ACTIVITY · Give your child five buttons. Have your child take away two buttons and tell how many are left.

Name _____

Subtract on a Ten Frame

red	red	red	red	red
red	red	red	red	red

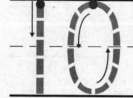 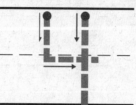 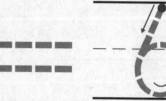

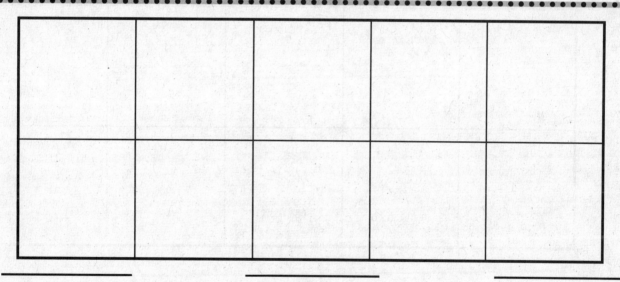

_____   _____

- - - - -   - - - - -
                         - - - - -

_____   _____

DIRECTIONS 1. Place 10 counters as shown on the ten frame. Take away 4 counters. Trace the circle around the set of counters that you took away. Trace the X on that set. Trace the subtraction sentence. 2. Place 10 counters on the ten frame. Draw the counters. Take away some counters. Circle the set of counters that you took away. Mark an X on that set. Complete the subtraction sentence.

Getting Ready for Grade 1   two hundred eighty-one **P281**

3

<table>
<tr><td></td><td></td><td></td><td></td><td></td></tr>
<tr><td></td><td></td><td></td><td></td><td></td></tr>
</table>

_____   _____   _____

– – – – –   ▬▬▬▬   – – – – –   ▬▬▬▬   – – – – –
                                         ▬▬▬▬
_____   _____   _____

· ·

4

<table>
<tr><td></td><td></td><td></td><td></td><td></td></tr>
<tr><td></td><td></td><td></td><td></td><td></td></tr>
</table>

_____   _____

– – – – –   ▬▬▬▬   – – – – –   ▬▬▬▬
                                 ▬▬▬▬
_____   _____

· ·

DIRECTIONS 3–4. Place 10 counters on the ten frame. Draw the counters. Take away some counters. Circle the set of counters that you took away. Mark an X on that set. Complete the subtraction sentence.

HOME ACTIVITY • Give your child ten household objects, such as buttons. Have your child take some of the objects away. Then have him or her write the subtraction sentence.

Name _____

Algebra: Missing Part

Whole
2

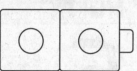

Part	Part
2	0
1	
0	

Whole
3

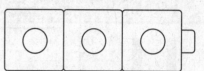

Part	Part
3	
2	
1	
0	

DIRECTIONS 1–2. How many cubes in all? Complete the chart to show the missing part that makes the whole.

Getting Ready for Grade 1

two hundred eighty-three **P283**

3

Whole	
4	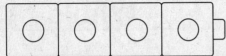

Part	Part
4	___
3	___
2	___
1	___
0	___

4

Whole	
5	

Part	Part
5	___
4	___
3	___
2	___
1	___
0	___

DIRECTIONS   3–4. How many cubes in all? Complete the chart to show the missing part that makes the whole.

HOME ACTIVITY • Place 8 spoons on the table. Cover 3 of the spoons. Tell your child that you started with 8 spoons. Ask him or her to tell you how many spoons are under the sheet of paper.

P284 two hundred eighty-four

Subtraction Sentences

1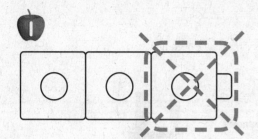

$$3 - 1 = 2$$

2

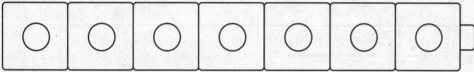

$$7 - \underline{\quad} = 3$$

3

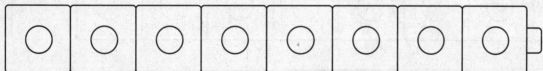

$$8 - \underline{\quad} = 5$$

DIRECTIONS **1.** How many cubes in all? Trace the cube being taken away. Trace to complete the subtraction sentence. **2–3.** What number is missing in the subtraction sentence? Circle and mark an X to show that number. Write the number to complete the subtraction sentence.

Getting Ready for Grade 1

two hundred eighty-five **P285**

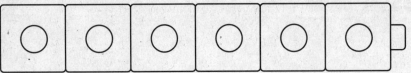

$$6 - \underline{\quad} = 4$$

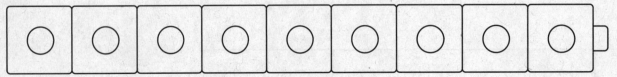

$$9 - \underline{\quad} = 6$$

$$10 - \underline{\quad} = 5$$

DIRECTIONS 4–6. What number is missing in the subtraction sentence? Circle and mark an X to show that number. Write the number to complete the subtraction sentence.

HOME ACTIVITY • Use self-stick notes or small pieces of paper to write subtraction sentences as shown above. Have your child fill in the missing number to complete the subtraction sentence.

Subtract to Compare

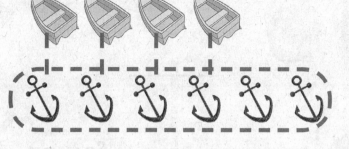

 **2** more

_____
- - - - - -
_____ more

_____
- - - - - -
_____ more

© Houghton Mifflin Harcourt

DIRECTIONS **1.** Trace the lines to match the objects in the top row to the objects in the bottom row. Compare the sets. Trace the circle that shows the set with more objects. Trace the number. **2–3.** Draw lines to match the objects in the top row to the objects in the bottom row. Compare the sets. Circle the set that has more objects. Write how many more.

Getting Ready for Grade 1

4

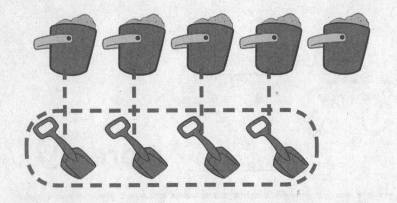

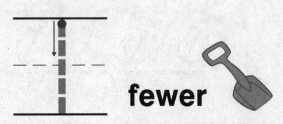

fewer

5

_____

- - - - - - -

_____ **fewer**

6

_____

- - - - - - -

_____ **fewer**

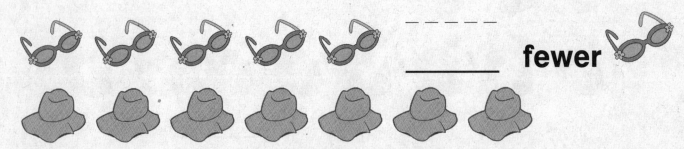

DIRECTIONS 4. Trace the lines to match the objects in the top row to the objects in the bottom row. Compare the sets. Trace the circle that shows the set with fewer objects. Trace the number. **5–6.** Draw lines to match the objects in the top row to the objects in the bottom row. Compare the sets. Circle the set that has fewer objects. Write how many fewer.

HOME ACTIVITY • Show your child a row of seven pennies and a row of three nickels. Have your child compare the sets, identify which has fewer coins, and tell how many fewer. Repeat with other sets of coins up to ten.

Name _____

Concepts and Skills

2 -‑ _____ ═══ ─‑‑‑‑

_____ ‑‑‑ _____ ‑‑‑‑ ═══ _____

© Houghton Mifflin Harcourt Publishing Company

DIRECTIONS 1. Use cubes to show the number. Draw the cubes. Take away one cube. Circle the cube that you took away and mark an X on it. Complete the subtraction sentence. **(pp. P277–P278) 2.** Place 10 counters on the ten frame. Draw the counters. Take away some counters. Circle and mark an X on the counters that you took away. Complete the subtraction sentence. **(pp. P281–P282)**

3

_____ _____ _____ _____

_ _ _ _ _ _   ———   _ _ _ _ _ _   ===   _ _ _ _ _

_____ _____ _____ _____

4

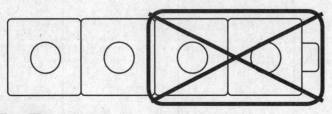

$$5 \;-\; \underline{\quad} \;=\; 3$$

5

$$4 \;-\; \underline{\quad} \;=\; 2$$

4 ○   3 ○   2 ○   I ○

DIRECTIONS **3.** Count and write how many boats in all. Two boats leave. Circle and mark an X on those boats. Complete the subtraction sentence. **(pp. P279–P280)** **4.** What number is missing in the subtraction sentence? Circle and mark an X to show that number. Write the number to complete the subtraction sentence. **(pp. P285–P286)** **5.** Mark under the number that is missing in the subtraction sentence. **(pp. P285–P286)**

Name _____

Order Numbers to 30

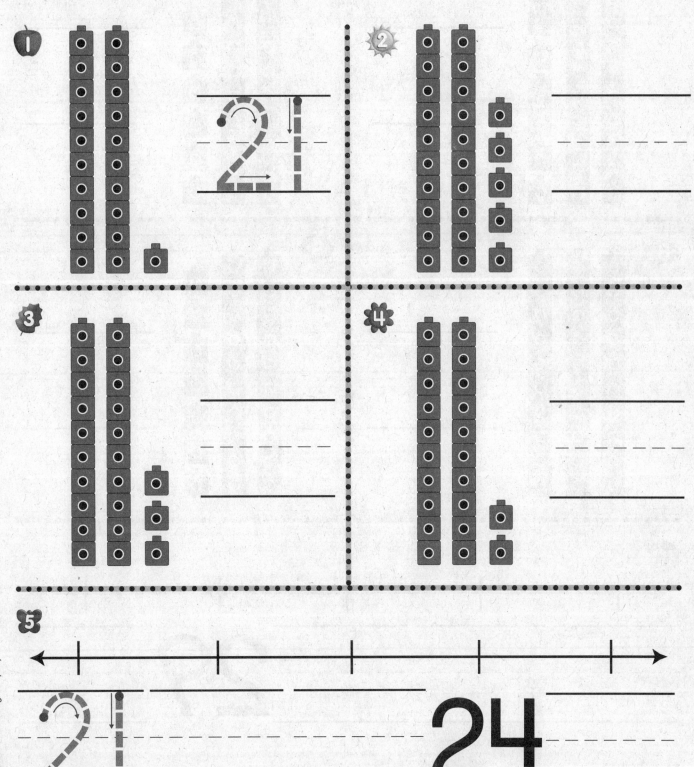

DIRECTIONS 1. Count the cubes. Trace the number.
2–4. Count the cubes. Write the number. **5.** Write those numbers in order on the number line.

Getting Ready for Grade 1

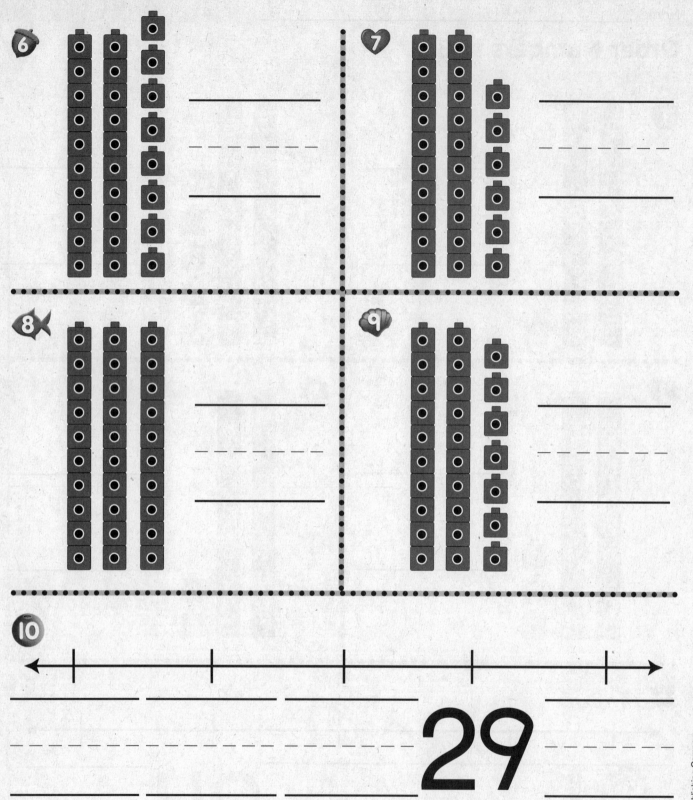

DIRECTIONS **6–9.** Count the cubes. Write the number. **10.** Write those numbers in order on the number line.

HOME ACTIVITY • Ask your child to count aloud from 1 to 30. Then say a number between 1 and 29, and ask your child to tell what numbers come before and after it.

Name _____

Skip Count by Twos

1	2	3	4	5	6	7	8	9	10
11	12	13	14	15	16	17	18	19	20
21	22	23	24	25	26	27	28	29	30
31	32	33	34	35	36	37	38	39	40

DIRECTIONS   1 Build 20 two-cube trains. Place a two-cube train on the 2, 4, 6, 8, 10, 12, and 14. Continue placing two-cube trains to finish the pattern up to 40. Touch each cube train as you count by twos.

Getting Ready for Grade 1

two hundred ninety-three **P293**

1	2	3	4	5	6	7	8	9	10
11	12	13	14	15	16	17	18	19	20
21	22	23	24	25	26	27	28	29	30
31	32	33	34	35	36	37	38	39	40
41	42	43	44	45	46	47	48	49	50
51	52	53	54	55	56	57	58	59	60
61	62	63	64	65	66	67	68	69	70
71	72	73	74	75	76	77	78	79	80
81	82	83	84	85	86	87	88	89	90
91	92	93	94	95	96	97	98	99	100

DIRECTIONS 2. Color the numbers that you say when you count by twos. Touch the numbers that you colored as you count by twos.

HOME ACTIVITY • Help your child practice counting by twos.

Name _____

Skip Count by Fives

1	2	3	4	5	6	7	8	9	10
11	12	13	14	15	16	17	18	19	20
21	22	23	24	25	26	27	28	29	30
31	32	33	34	35	36	37	38	39	40
41	42	43	44	45	46	47	48	49	50

DIRECTIONS   1. Build 10 five-cube towers. Place a five-cube tower on all the numbers that end in 5 or a 0. Touch each cube tower as you count by fives.

Getting Ready for Grade 1

1	2	3	4	5	6	7	8	9	10
11	12	13	14	15	16	17	18	19	20
21	22	23	24	25	26	27	28	29	30
31	32	33	34	35	36	37	38	39	40
41	42	43	44	45	46	47	48	49	50
51	52	53	54	55	56	57	58	59	60
61	62	63	64	65	66	67	68	69	70
71	72	73	74	75	76	77	78	79	80
81	82	83	84	85	86	87	88	89	90
91	92	93	94	95	96	97	98	99	100

DIRECTIONS   2. Color each number that ends in a 5 or a 0. Touch the numbers you colored as you count by fives.

HOME ACTIVITY • Help your child practice counting by fives.

© Houghton Mifflin Harcourt Publishing Company

Tally Marks

Set	Number	Tally Marks
	5	
	_____ - - - - - _____	
	_____ - - - - - _____	

DIRECTIONS Look at the model at the top of the page that shows a set, the number, and tally marks. **1–2.** Write how many in the set. Draw the tally marks to show the same number.

Set	Number	Tally Marks
3	_____ - - - - - - _____	
4	_____ - - - - - - _____	
5	_____ - - - - - - _____	

DIRECTIONS 3–5. Write how many in the set. Draw the tally marks to show the same number.

HOME ACTIVITY · Give your child up to 10 household objects, such as buttons. Have him or her use tally marks to show how many buttons.

Name _____

Skip Count by Tens

1	2	3	4	5	6	7	8	9	10
11	12	13	14	15	16	17	18	19	20
21	22	23	24	25	26	27	28	29	30
31	32	33	34	35	36	37	38	39	40
41	42	43	44	45	46	47	48	49	50
51	52	53	54	55	56	57	58	59	60
61	62	63	64	65	66	67	68	69	70
71	72	73	74	75	76	77	78	79	80
81	82	83	84	85	86	87	88	89	90
91	92	93	94	95	96	97	98	99	100

DIRECTIONS 1. Color each number that ends in 0. Point to each number you colored as you skip count by tens.

Getting Ready for Grade 1

② 10, 20, 30, 40, 50

③ 30, ____, 50, ____, 70

④ 10, ____, ____, 40, 50

⑤ 50, ____, 70, ____, 90

⑥ 60, ____, 80, ____, 100

DIRECTIONS **2.** Skip count by tens. Trace the numbers. **3–6.** Skip count by tens. Write the missing numbers.

HOME ACTIVITY • Give your child objects in bundles of 10, such as toothpicks or straws. Have your child count the objects by tens.

Name _____

Skip Count Coins

 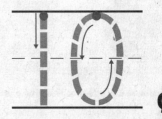
¢

¢

¢

¢

¢

DIRECTIONS 1–5. How many dimes? Skip count by tens. Write how many cents.

Getting Ready for Grade 1

6

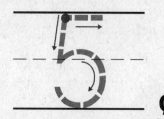

_____
_____ ¢

7

_____
- - - - - - -
_____ ¢

8

_____
- - - - - - -
_____ ¢

9

_____
- - - - - - -
_____ ¢

10

_____
- - - - - - -
_____ ¢

DIRECTIONS 6–10. How many nickels? Skip count by fives. Write how many cents.

HOME ACTIVITY • Give your child some nickels. Have him or her practice skip counting by fives.

© Houghton Mifflin Harcourt Publishing Company

Name _____

Concepts and Skills

1

_____

- - - - - - - - - -

_____

2

_____

- - - - - - - - - -

_____

3

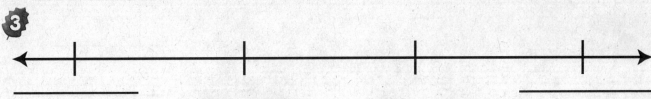

_____   _____

- - - - - - - - - -   - - - - - - - - - -

4

1	2	3	4	5	6	7	8	9	10
11	12	13	14	15	16	17	18	19	20
21	22	23	24	25	26	27	28	29	30
31	32	33	34	35	36	37	38	39	40
41	42	43	44	45	46	47	48	49	50

DIRECTIONS   1–2. Count the cubes. Write the number. **(pp. P291–P292)**
3. Write those numbers in order on the number line. **(pp. P291–P292)**
4. Color each number that ends in a 5 or a 0. Skip count by fives. **(pp. P295–P296)**

5	Set	Number	Tally Marks
	● ● ● ● ● ● ● ● ●	___ - - - - ___	

6									
1	2	3	4	5	6	7	8	9	10
11	12	13	14	15	16	17	18	19	20
21	22	23	24	25	26	27	28	29	30

7

___
- - - -
___ ¢

8

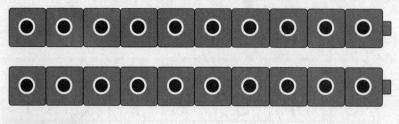

21   22   23   24

○   ○   ○   ○

DIRECTIONS **5.** Write how many in the set. Draw the tally marks to show the same number. (pp. P297–P298) **6.** Color the numbers that you say when you count by twos. (pp. P293–P294) **7.** How many dimes? Skip count by tens. Write how many cents. (pp. P301–P302) **8.** Count the cubes. Mark under the number that shows how many. (pp. P291–P292)

Name _____

Algebra: Extend a Growing Pattern

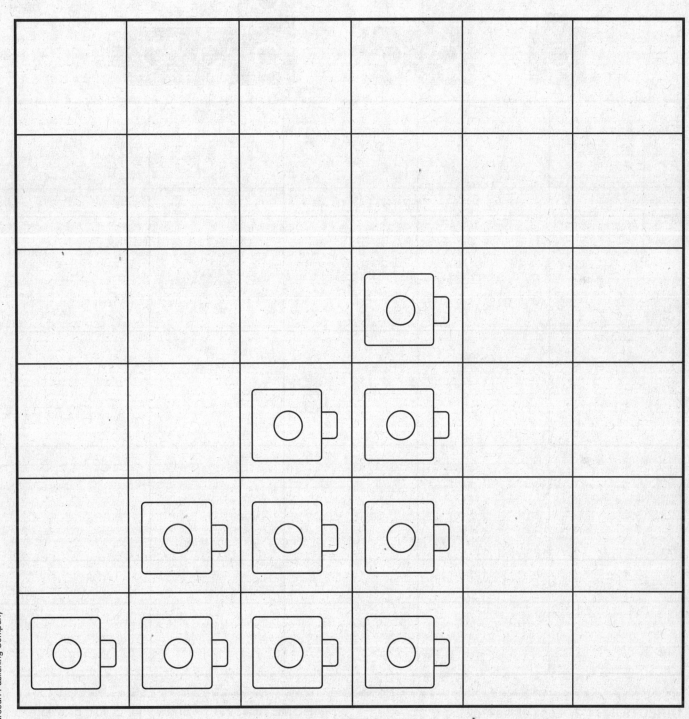

· ·

DIRECTIONS   **1.** Look at the pattern. Describe the pattern. Use connecting cubes to extend the pattern. Draw and color the cubes.

Getting Ready for Grade 1

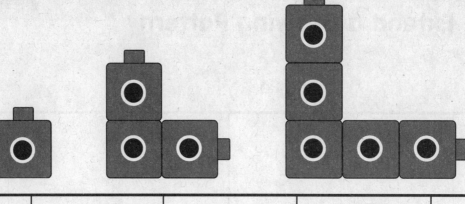

DIRECTIONS **2.** Look at the growing pattern at the top of the page. Place cubes on the grid to show what would come next in the growing pattern. Draw and color the cubes.

HOME ACTIVITY • Show your child a growing pattern using toothpicks. First, build a square with one toothpick on each side of the square. Then, build a square with two toothpicks on each side of the square, and another with three toothpicks on each side of the square. Have your child build the next square in the pattern.

Explore Measuring Tools

1

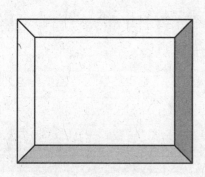

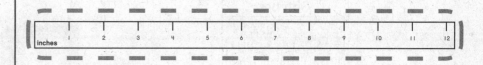

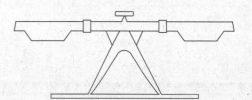

2

9 o'clock
10 o'clock
11 o'clock
12 o'clock
1 o'clock
2 o'clock
3 o'clock Dance Class   Dance Class
4 o'clock
5 o'clock

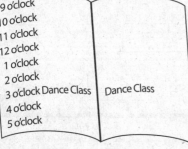

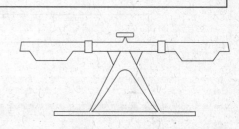

3

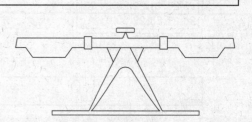

DIRECTIONS **1.** Look at the picture on the left. Trace the circle around the correct tool to measure the length of the picture frame.
2. Circle the correct tool to measure what time to be at dance class.
3. Circle the correct tool to measure which piece of fruit is heavier.

Getting Ready for Grade 1

inches | 1 | 2 | 3 | 4 | 5 | 6 | 7 | 8 | 9 | 10 | 11 | 12

October

Sunday	Monday	Tuesday	Wednesday	Thursday	Friday	Saturday
			1	2	3	4
5	6	7	8	9	10	11
12	13	14	15	16	17	18
19	20	21	22	23	24	25
26	27	28	29	30	31	

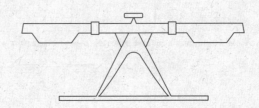

inches | 1 | 2 | 3 | 4 | 5 | 6 | 7 | 8 | 9 | 10 | 11 | 12

October

Sunday	Monday	Tuesday	Wednesday	Thursday	Friday	Saturday
			1	2	3	4
5	6	7	8	9	10	11
12	13	14	15	16	17	18
19	20	21	22	23	24	25
26	27	28	29	30	31	

inches | 1 | 2 | 3 | 4 | 5 | 6 | 7 | 8 | 9 | 10 | 11 | 12

DIRECTIONS 4. Circle the tool used to find the date. **5.** Circle the tool used to compare the weights of two objects. **6.** Circle the tool used to tell the time.

HOME ACTIVITY • Ask your child to describe the tool used to identify the months in a year.

Use a Clock

 1

 o'clock

---

 2

_____ o'clock

 3

_____ o'clock

 4

_____ o'clock

DIRECTIONS **1.** About what time does the clock show?
Trace the number. **2–4.** About what time does the clock show?
Write your answer.

| before 6 o'clock | about 6 o'clock | after 6 o'clock |

5

before 2 o'clock

about 2 o'clock

after 2 o'clock

6

before 7 o'clock

about 7 o'clock

after 7 o'clock

7

before 11 o'clock

about 11 o'clock

after 11 o'clock

DIRECTIONS   5–7. Circle the time shown on the watch.

HOME ACTIVITY • Look at or draw a simple clock. Ask your child questions such as: *Where does the hour hand go to show about 8 o'clock? About 1 o'clock? About 4 o'clock?*

© Houghton Mifflin Harcourt Publishing Company

Name _____

Concepts and Skills

  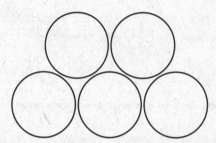

• •

 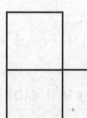 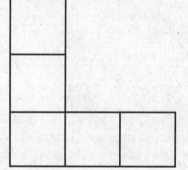

DIRECTIONS 1. Look at the pattern. Describe the pattern. Use counters to extend the pattern. Draw the counters. **(pp. P305–P306) 2.** Look at the pattern. Describe the pattern. Draw to show what would come next in the pattern. **(pp. P305–P306)**

3

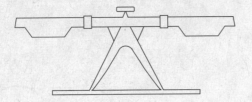

October

Sunday	Monday	Tuesday	Wednesday	Thursday	Friday	Saturday
			1	2	3	4
5	6	7	8	9	10	11
12	13	14	15	16	17	18
19	20	21	22	23	24	25
26	27	28	29	30	31	

4

_____

– – – – – – – –

about _____ o'clock

5

before 10 o'clock

about 10 o'clock

after 10 o'clock

6

○ about 2 o'clock   ○ about 3 o'clock

○ about 4 o'clock   ○ about 5 o'clock

DIRECTIONS **3.** Circle the tool used to find a holiday. **(pp. P307–P308)** **4.** About what time does the clock show? Write your answer. **(pp. P309–P310)** **5.** Circle the time shown on the watch **(pp. P309–P310)** **6.** About what time does the clock show? Mark beside your answer. **(pp. P309–P310)**